Riding for Deliveroo

Riding for Deliveroo

Resistance in the New Economy

Callum Cant

polity

First published in 2020 by Polity Press

Polity Press
65 Bridge Street
Cambridge CB2 1UR, UK

Polity Press
101 Station Landing
Suite 300
Medford, MA 02155, USA

ISBN-13: 978-1-5095-3550-7
ISBN-13: 978-1-5095-3551-4 (pb)

A catalogue record for this book is available from the British Library.

Library of Congress Cataloging-in-Publication Data
Names: Cant, Callum, author.
Title: Riding for Deliveroo : resistance in the new economy / Callum Cant.
Description: Cambridge, UK ; Medford, MA : Polity Press, 2019. | Includes
    bibliographical references. | Summary: "What is life like for workers in
    the gig economy? Is it a paradise of flexibility and freedom? Or is it a
    world of exploitation? Callum Cant took a job with one of the most
    prominent platforms, Deliveroo, to find out. This mix of first-hand
    testimony and analysis is essential for anyone wishing to understand
    class struggle in platform capitalism"-- Provided by publisher.
Identifiers: LCCN 2019009985 (print) | LCCN 2019980167 (ebook) | ISBN
    9781509535507 (hardback) | ISBN 9781509535514 (paperback) | ISBN
    9781509535521 (epub)
Subjects: LCSH: Deliveroo (Firm)--Employees. | Express
    service--Employees--Great Britain. | Express service--Employees--Labor
    unions--Great Britain. | Self-employed--Great Britain. | Employee
    rights--Great Britain.
Classification: LCC HD8039.E82 G733 2019 (print) | LCC HD8039.E82 (ebook)
    | DDC 331.7/613831830941--dc23
LC record available at https://lccn.loc.gov/2019009985
LC ebook record available at https://lccn.loc.gov/2019980167

Typeset in 11 on 14 pt Sabon by
Servis Filmsetting Ltd, Stockport, Cheshire
Printed and bound in Great Britain by CPI Group (UK) Ltd, Croydon

For further information on Polity, visit our website: politybooks.com

Contents

Acknowledgements

I received invaluable support whilst writing this book, for which I am very grateful, particularly from my Ph.D. supervisors, Helen Hester and Jamie Woodcock. I am indebted to the workers, in Brighton and elsewhere, whose creativity and bravery are the source of everything worth reading herein. And, finally, I owe huge thanks to Ev, my team mate.

Preface: London, August 2016

In the summer of 2016, the UK Border Agency (UKBA) was paying close attention to restaurants in London. By late July, they had homed in on twelve branches of Byron Burgers across London. Workers at these branches were told by their managers they had to attend a 10.30 a.m. meeting on the proper cooking of burgers before the lunch shift started – in fact, they were attending an immigration raid. Around twenty workers were detained and then deported.

News of the raid began to spread amongst a group of workers who knew the deported staff well and had similar experiences of their own: Deliveroo couriers. They were outraged at the collaboration between managers and UKBA. Just a few weeks before, Deliveroo had also worked with the UKBA to 'assist in a documentation check' at their own Islington HQ, which resulted in three workers being detained. If companies were happy to profit off the work of migrants, the argument went, then they should not sell them down the river as soon as the Border Agency called. An idea for action spread rapidly amongst the couriers – they would all refuse to deliver Byron Burger orders. For the first time, they were taking collective action.

Two weeks later, Deliveroo announced that they were going to change the way workers in London were paid. The system would be changed from a flat hourly rate (£7) with a bonus per completed delivery (£1) plus an additional petrol bonus for moped riders, to a fee-per-delivery piece-wage (£3.75) with no hourly rate. If there were no orders, workers would earn no money. For many, this change amounted to a pay cut, but management predicted it would offer Deliveroo significant savings during down times. What they did not predict, however, was what would happen next.

Hundreds of workers across the city began a strike. They organized huge roving demonstrations of mopeds and cyclists that converged upon Deliveroo's central London office. The service was in chaos, with orders going undelivered all over the city. The Independent Workers of Great Britain (IWGB), a London-based grassroots union, launched a crowd-funder to help support workers during the strike. Within days it had raised over £20,000. As a result, workers could now pay themselves a basic wage for the duration. The decision was made to stay out for another day, and then another. On the third day of the strike, Dan Warne, managing director of Deliveroo UK, decided to talk to the strikers. Every day, the crowd gathering on the steps opposite the head office seemed to be getting bigger. Now it was in the hundreds. A worker filmed what happened next.

It's a hot, sunny day, and Dan walks out of the office, across the road and right up to the crowd, holding a straight face all the time. A few strikers heckle him, but they let him walk into the crowd. On the steps is a group of IWGB members who are there to support the strike. At the head of the group is Max Dewhurst, a CitySprint courier and experienced trade unionist. They start to smile. They can tell what is coming next.

Dan clears his throat. The workers close the circle around him and start to shout and laugh. Those standing at the top of the steps loom over him. He gestures for the workers to be quiet. He starts to speak: 'Can I have some silence, ladies and gents . . .' The company, he says, is willing to listen to every worker's concerns, individually. The response is not positive. The workers want collective bargaining, and they tell him as much, at full volume. One worker steps forward: 'Everyone wants the same thing: £8 per hour, plus £1 per drop. That's it.' Dan responds, 'Listen guys, there needs to be an explanation around what the changes are, it's a change in payment method, not lower wages . . .' The workers cut him off. They tell him that's not what they want. He tries again, 'That is a dialogue we will have individually. So, where we have done this, first of all, this is a trial . . .' Another roar. The workers show him their signs, on which their demands are clearly written down. 'Look at it!' Everyone wants the same thing: £8 per hour, plus £1 per drop. That's it.

For the first time, Dan Warne, the managing director of Deliveroo UK, is face to face with organized couriers, who actually do the work for Deliveroo UK. The thousands of dots on the map, spread all over London, are showing that they are real people with real power. From the back of the crowd, a chant starts: 'Out, out, out, out!' Soon everyone is shouting together. Dan looks left and right. He steps back, turns, and walks away, back into the office. The crowd cheers as he goes.

The strike ended four days later. By that time, the workers' demands had increased – they wanted the London living wage (£8.25) per hour, plus costs, plus a bonus per delivery. They settled for a compromise position of the status quo, with the existing workers keeping a £7 per hour plus £1 per drop payment structure. It was only a partial victory. All new workers would be put on the new per-drop-only payment structure. Despite a large proportion of the strikers joining the IWGB and demanding it lead negotiations, Deliveroo continued to refuse to participate in formal collective bargaining or to allow trade union representation. Deliveroo continued to maintain the legal fiction that its couriers were 'independent contractors'. But that strike was the beginning of something. Deliveroo workers had shown they could take on their bosses – and, from London, the fight would spread, across the UK, Europe, and, finally, the world.

1

Introduction

Deliveroo is a food-delivery platform. That means different things depending on where you stand. From the point of view of the customer, it is an app which charges you a fee to deliver restaurant food to your home. From the point of view of the restaurant owner, it is a bolt-on outsourced delivery service that takes a cut of the value of all delivery orders. For the couriers, it is an app you work for which pays you to take food from restaurants to customers. For investors, it is an app you pump hundreds of millions of pounds into, in the hope it will eventually turn a profit.

Anyone who lives in, works in, or visits a major British city will be familiar with the blur of Deliveroo couriers rushing food through traffic or standing around on pavements. The company was founded in London in February 2013 by Will Shu and Greg Orlowski and has gone on to expand globally. Between 2013 and 2016, Deliveroo's revenue grew by 107,117 per cent – that is, one hundred and seven thousand, one hundred and seventeen per cent – making it the number one fastest-growing company in Europe over that period, by far.[1]

This rapid expansion has been based on abundant investor capital, which has allowed Deliveroo to rack up huge losses.[2] Whilst Deliveroo's total revenue increased 611 per cent in 2016, with sales of £128.6 million, it also recorded a loss of £129.1 million.[3] In 2017, those losses widened to £185 million as the company continued to plough money into rapid growth.[4] Even looking past the expansion plan, Deliveroo's margins remain tight. Delivery costs for 2016 were £127.5 million, just £1.1 million less than total sales. Despite only paying its couriers poverty wages, the platform's profit margins were smaller than 1 per cent, although Deliveroo claims that mature markets are significantly more profitable. The platform is a prime example of how the 'gig economy' relies on huge bubbles of investment to create global start-ups with disruptive models, limited profitability, and exploitative practices.

Every day, thousands of Deliveroo couriers work delivering food in towns and cities across the UK. This book is about them and the reality of their work, behind the glossy exterior of the app. To hear CEO Will Shu talk about Deliveroo, you would think it was a company defined by innovation, entrepreneurship, and flexibility. But from the point of view of workers, it's more about low pay, precarious conditions, and conflict. This is not just a sob story about workers being exploited in bad conditions by bosses who get rich off their work – it's also about how workers have squared up and fought back.

Introduction

Workers and Bosses

That contradiction between workers and bosses is a class contradiction. But what is a class? Classes are social groups defined by their antagonistic economic relationships to one another. By their very nature, classes are always in more or less organized conflict with one another, and this conflict shapes society. The class which dominates society and all the other classes in that conflict is called the ruling class. Because this class is dominant, it gets to organize society to suit its interests. In a capitalist society, the majority of people belong to one of two classes: bosses or workers.

Bosses are the ruling class of capitalist society, and are defined by the fact that they own and control the ability and the means to produce the stuff that everyone else needs in order to survive. They use this ability to produce huge amounts of value, by selling things which workers produce back to workers as commodities. As such, they turn the means of producing useful things into a way of making profit, otherwise known as 'capital'. Some of these bosses are CEOs, whilst others are just investors or landlords who let other people run the nuts and bolts of exploitation but take a share of the profit anyway. In order to maintain this system based on profit for the few and scarcity for the many, bosses have to stay on top. To do so, they use the power they derive from their control of the economy to capture parts of the state and other social institutions

Workers are defined by the fact that they have to work in order to survive. Being a worker means spending most of your life making someone else rich. They

3

make up the vast majority of society, but do not benefit from the way it is organized and run. Without workers, capitalism would be impossible, but capitalism is not in workers' interests.

Only a social revolution can fully resolve this contradiction, by getting rid of capitalist social relations and replacing them with something else. As a result, organized workers have generally spent the last 170-odd years aiming for a different kind of society from capitalism, one which would benefit them: *socialism*.

However, the ruling class is opposed to any transformation of society. It is precisely those class contradictions of capitalism that they rely upon for their profits. So, the ruling class are always interested in maintaining capitalism, no matter how badly things might be going – they do not even want to solve the problem. So, when organized workers fight for socialism, they end up in a class struggle with their bosses. This struggle has shaped the world we live in today. Working-class victories include weekends, the NHS, the limits on the length of the working day, an end to child labour, and the ability to vote. But whilst workers have succeeded in changing the form of capitalism we live under, they have not yet got rid of capitalism altogether. Nonetheless, the working class is the only class capable of acting in the interests of everyone and abolishing class-divided society forever. The only other alternative is to continue on in a system that is coming apart at the seams.

In-between these two struggling classes are all sorts of other groups with their own specific interests. Bureaucrats, shop owners, leftover aristocrats and the rest are part of neither of the predominant classes, but most of the time, apart from when things are going really badly, they throw their weight behind the ruling class.

The analysis of class proposed by the establishment is the complete opposite of the argument above. For mainstream liberals, capitalist society isn't made up of two opposed classes at all. Instead, it is a jumble of property-owning individuals. These individuals, whether bosses or workers, all have a universal common interest in a system that maintains the rule of private property above all else. For them, capitalist society isn't class against class – it's a deathmatch, all against all, with a consistent set of rules.

As a result, liberals think that the people who make up the ruling class are legitimately successful entrepreneurs. They've out-competed everyone else and risen to the top because they're the best and they work the hardest. Workers, on the other hand, are lazy. They are playing the same game as the bosses under the same rules, they are just not very good at it. After all, if a worker is stuck in a low-paying job, they could always just get another – it is a free society.

Karl Marx's response to this argument is as accurate now as it was in the nineteenth century. Yes, workers are 'free' – they are 'free' to sell their labour-power to an employer, and they are 'free' of any ability to survive if they don't get paid. Once workers have sold their labour-power, it is then used by their boss to produce commodities. These commodities are worth more than the value paid back to the worker in wages. This extra 'surplus value' is either reinvested by the boss, redistributed to other members of the ruling class through rent, interest and dividends, or converted into profit. In reality, capitalism gives workers no choice: they have to sell their labour-power in order to get a wage and buy the stuff, the commodities, they need to survive. They can stop working for any one capitalist and go and get another job, but they can never stop working for the capitalist class altogether. You work and are exploited to make your boss rich, or you starve – some 'freedom'.[5]

It's not unusual to hear pundits argue that people who understand class as Marx did are living in the past. In the new 'sharing economy', everyone is a winner, they say. But that same struggle between workers and bosses that has defined the last two centuries of our history still defines it today. Society is still predominantly divided into two camps: that small group of people who live off the value produced by others, and that big group of people whose only choice is to work or starve. It doesn't matter whether that system is organized by telegraph or by app, it's still capitalism.

The question is, do you see the 2,208 billionaires who run the world as a ruling class, or as legitimately successful business people who just worked harder than the billions of people living in absolute poverty? This book takes Marx's side. So, it is written from the perspective of the working class: the class which has nothing to lose but its chains. In order to do so, it is based on research carried out through a method called 'workers' inquiry'.

Workers' Inquiry

The term 'workers' inquiry' comes from a 101-question survey written by Marx in 1880 and distributed to workers and socialists across France. Late in his life, Marx argued that only workers really understood the concrete reality of capitalism, and that socialists had to gain an *'exact and positive* knowledge of the conditions in which the working class – the class to whom the future belongs – works and moves'.[6] This research wasn't just about finding things out for the fun of it. In 1845, Friedrich Engels, Marx's close friend, co-author, and editor, wrote *The condition of the working class in England*.[7] It was based on extensive research in Manchester into the social crisis facing the emerging British working class. Engels hoped to appeal to the bosses, the capitalist ruling class, to recognize the problems created by the industrial revolution and make some changes as a result. Marx's workers' inquiry, however, had a different approach. Rather than appealing to the ruling class's better nature, Marx wanted to actively learn from that class to whom the future belongs and help out on their side of the class struggle. The goal of this struggle was to 'expropriate the expropriators', boot the bosses out of power, and reorganize society from the bottom up.[8]

Workers' inquiry has been used on and off by different parts of the socialist movement ever since. Three currents, active between the late 1950s and the 1970s, played a particularly important role in developing the method beyond Marx.[9] The first was the Johnson–Forest Tendency, a group of unorthodox American socialists who developed workers' inquiry in the form of narratives. They collected stories of everyday working-class life, which they hoped would help provoke class consciousness amongst their readership. The second is Socialism or Barbarism (*Socialisme ou Barbarie*), a French group who helped produce a workers' newspaper (*Tribune Ouvrière*) in the Alcatraz-lookalike Renault

Billancourt factory, built on an island in the Seine slap-bang in the middle of the 'Red Belt' of working-class suburbs that surround Paris. The third and final group is Italian Workerism (*Operaismo*). Workerism was less unified but in many ways more influential than either the Johnson–Forest Tendency or Socialism or Barbarism. It contained a range of perspectives, from relatively straight-laced socialists to anarcho-sociologists. The project that united them all was an attempt to use workers' inquiry to relaunch socialist politics in a period where the working class looked increasingly detached from the trade unions and political parties that had historically represented it. Whereas classical sociological research into work had been conducted from the point of view of the bosses, with the goal of increasing profits, the workerists wanted to turn it on its head. In the most revolutionary parts of the current, they would use sociology to look for the points of attack where the working class could launch an offensive on capitalism, as the 'centre' of Italian politics fell apart.

This book uses workers' inquiry in a similar way to the workerists. I have learnt about Deliveroo and the conflicts within it from the workers' point of view. I worked for Deliveroo part-time in Brighton for eight months and, with hundreds of other workers, organized a union branch and a series of strikes and protests for better pay and conditions. That experience is the basis of what follows. In the process of writing, I've also interviewed workers from the UK and helped compile a self-reported workers' database, produced by a European network, on the spread of strikes and protests in food platforms. Taken together, this research, for the first time, tells the comprehensive story of strikes and

Introduction

worker resistance in the gig economy from the perspective of the workers themselves.

Class Composition

Workers' inquiry is not enough on its own. Collecting information from the workers' point of view is important, but information means nothing if it's not interpreted. Whenever someone goes from raw information to specific arguments, they use a set of theoretical principles and assumptions about how the world works. If the theoretical principles are no good, then the resulting argument is no good. Imagine an apple falls on your head – that information could mean a lot of different things, depending on how you understand the world: either it could mean it's raining apples, or it could mean gravity exists. Within workerism, this progression from raw information to analysis had a close connection with a particular theory: class composition.

Class composition is a Marxist theory that focuses on changes in the balance of power between classes over time, and how shifts in the organization of work and society impact on the form of class conflict. Analysis that uses class composition theory pays attention to the relationship between three particular areas: the first is the organization of individual workers into a productive workforce (technical composition); the second is the organization of workers into a class-based society outside of work (social composition); the third is the self-organization of the working class into a force for class conflict (political composition). In short, the class composition of a workplace has three parts: the work, the workers, and the workers' organization.[10] In periods of rapid technological, social, and political change, it focuses on understanding huge processes of transformation via their material roots in the everyday lives of normal people.

And what is our situation today if not one of rapid change? In the 1990s, the common-sense assumption of global politics was that we were living in the 'end of history'.[11] The Soviet Union had been defeated, the cold war was over, and the system of liberal capitalist democracy was going to ensure a new golden era of growth and stability. Global elites settled in, expecting a comfy ride. But in 2007–8, global capitalism fell victim to one of its inevitable crises. In the long depression that followed, we saw the end of the end of history.[12] Something had to change, fast. The response of global elites was an all-out economic assault on the working class. Bail-outs, labour deregulation, resource privatization, environmental exploitation, and social austerity – that was the only way for capitalism to be saved. But it was saved at the expense of ordinary people.

As a result of that assault, the political status quo went out the window. The comfy ride of ruling-class domination turned into a rollercoaster. Between 2010 and 2015, protests, strikes, social movements, and revolutions swept the world. What the cultural theorist Mark Fisher called 'capitalist realism' – the assumption that capitalism is the only way of organizing human social life – began to fall apart.[13] The technical and social composition of the working class had changed, and the political composition was transformed as a result.

Now, finally, the morbid symptoms of a collapsing consensus are obvious. If a well-paid political pundit says something is impossible, then it's probably going to happen within the next six months. Politics is polarizing fast. Our choice is between a society run by workers from the bottom up, with room for everyone – or deadly borders and impoverished communities watched over by a class of billionaire oligarchs.

In the middle of this chaos, we can only understand what it all means by paying attention to the everyday reality of life for the majority of people. For good or for bad, that's where the future will be decided. In the final analysis, workplaces and homes are more important than parliaments and TV studios. The centre cannot hold – what replaces it is up to us.

Why Deliveroo?

Paying attention to the everyday lives of workers has to start somewhere. In this book, it starts with Deliveroo. Deliveroo bears the marks of this wider crisis, whilst also being a ubiquitous part of urban life. But why pay attention to it specifically?

The first reason is because of the role Deliveroo plays in the development of capitalism. You hear a lot about Deliveroo in relation to something called the 'gig economy'. What exactly the 'gig economy' means isn't very clear. It is a term that lumps together all different kinds of changes to society which only seem to share two things: they all look a bit tech and they all seem a bit new. This book junks that category. Instead, it uses 'platform capitalism', an idea developed by Nick Srnicek.[14] The basic argument behind this change is that, rather than thinking about companies like Uber and Airbnb as *tech start-ups* with special *tech start-up* characteristics, we should think of them as *capitalist* companies with *capitalist* characteristics. Srnicek defines platforms as digital infrastructures which enable two or more groups to interact and extract data from that interaction. More specifically, Deliveroo is a geographically tethered platform. Geographically tethered platforms are distinct from other platforms because they sell a service that requires the workers who are providing that service to do their work in a specific place.[15] Despite using an app, Deliveroo is still a company that pays people to do a particular job in a particular place, and extracts value from them as they do so.

But geographically tethered platforms aren't yet viable capitalist companies. Without substantial investment from outside sources, they would go bust. These investors are taking a big bet that these platforms can become profitable at some point. But until Deliveroo starts bringing home big annual profits, it's a stretch to imagine that it, or companies like it, could lead a process of national or global economic growth. No one knows whether the investors' bet is going to come off.

As of February 2017, there were 15,000 couriers working for Deliveroo in the UK.[16] That's not an insignificant number, but it's still nowhere near the big players in sectors like retail, logistics, healthcare, manufacturing, or any other major part of the economy. Deliveroo has about as big a workforce as London Stansted Airport. But, as Srnicek argues, what matters is less the actual business performance of platforms or the size of their workforce, and more the way that they change the landscape of the wider economy.

Introduction

An analogy with computers is useful. Did computers matter for the development of capitalism because
computer manufacture became the largest sector in
the economy? Obviously not. Instead, computers have
been fundamentally important for capitalism because
they have become the universal tool that allows for
the mass reorganization of *other* work. The developments made in the early implementations of computer
technology opened the way for a much wider change.
Whilst those experiments were going on, there was a
brief opportunity to see how computers were going to
reorganize work and potentially spread that knowledge
from worker to worker.[17] Or we could take an even
older example: the assembly line. In the early nineteenth
century, Boston-based textile mills were the first factories to be reorganized around 'continuous flow' labour
processes. In these factories, the pace of work was set by
the machinery, not by individual workers. Here, almost
a century before the Ford motor company developed the
assembly line in car manufacture, was a chance to see
the future of the factory.[18] So, when new technology is
being implemented in the workplace, there is a critical
window of opportunity for adaptation. If workers can
spread information and tactics whilst this window is
open, the working class can gain a strategic advantage
over their bosses.

Just like computers and assembly lines, the developments made in platform capitalism may come to have
wide-reaching effects. In particular, the use of 'algorithmic management' to partially automate labour
process supervision and coordination could become an
increasingly common practice.[19] If this technology is to
be implemented for human benefit rather than profit,

13

workers need to be in control – and that means we need to develop the kind of tactics that could help us come out on top.

One of the oldest tactics of working-class power is the strike. The name comes from sailors 'striking' their topsails to immobilize their ships. The term first entered usage in 1768, when coal-heavers and sailors in London refused to load and move their ships in order to gain leverage over their bosses.[20] The striking of sails was an immediate, visual signal to everyone in the area that work was stopping, and something was going down. The power gained by collectively refusing to work has been associated with the word strike ever since.

But this development would only really kick in when the industrial revolution led to the total reorganization of British society. British workers were the first in the world to experience industrial capitalism – emerging, as Marx said, 'dripping from head to foot, from every pore, with blood and dirt'.[21] Peasants were cleared from the highlands, workers were starved in slum cities, and children worked with heavy machinery for hours and hours every day. But, from this dismal point, the forward march of labour began.

Due to Britain's early industrialization, it was the first country to see the emergence of a mass workers' movement. British workers began to organize and join trade unions, even when they faced being massacred by the state or deported to Australia as a result. These early workers wielded the strike as their most effective weapon. The most militant amongst them, like William Benbow, dreamt of a 'grand national holiday' when all workers would strike together to overthrow their oppressors, establish plenty, abolish want, and render all people equal through a new constitution drafted by a working-class government.[22]

This dream was never achieved, but the workers movement in Britain did grow into a colossal social force. Across the decades, workers came to the brink of changing everything, again and again. In 1926, a British general strike came too late to build on the revolutionary energy of the immediate post-war period, but still shook the ruling class to its core. In 1974, a coal miners' strike toppled the Tory government. Then, in 1979, the 'winter of discontent' saw 4,608,000 British workers recorded as going on strike – although the real number is likely to be higher. At least 18 per cent of the total economically active population was involved in strike action at some point in the year. But, soon after, the workers' movement stuttered.

That stutter then turned into a retreat, as the movement began to lose ground to a new offensive launched by the ruling class. The specifically British form of this global offensive was Thatcherism – that is to say, the Conservative politics of Margaret Thatcher. She pushed through a kind of 'authoritarian populism' based on the smashing of the organized working class and its trade unions, the repression of minorities (urban black and Asian communities and LGBT people, in particular), and a huge sell-off of state assets.[23] The economic form of this offensive was a 'neoliberal' reorganization of the state and the economy. David Harvey describes neoliberalism as: 'a theory of political economic practices that proposes that human well-being can best be advanced by liberating individual entrepreneurial freedoms and skills within an institutional framework characterised by strong private property rights, free markets and free

trade'.[24] That 'liberation', for workers, has meant losing
many of the protections against the most aggressive
forms of capitalism that they had won over the previous century. Neoliberalism is, in short, an economic
doctrine of class war from above. In the workplace,
British bosses regained the initiative through the reorganization of production via global logistics, the use of
new technology to reduce worker leverage, and cooperation with the state in the smashing of trade unionism
and introduction of restrictive new laws. Overall, the
development of neoliberalism in the UK led to mass
unemployment, the opening up of an increasingly large
inequality gap, and the erosion of the welfare state. This
combined assault was what cultural theorist Stuart Hall
characterized as the 'great moving right show'.[25]

The result of that successful attack is a modern workers' movement in decline. Since the crisis of 2008-9,
UK workers have fought their corner by protesting and
hell-raising, but they've rarely gone on strike.[26] Trade
unions are getting smaller, their membership is getting
older, and their bite is getting weaker. In 2017, only
30,000 workers went on strike – the smallest number
since records began in 1893.[27]

But in this context, with strikes in decline, Deliveroo
workers have launched a militant struggle for a better
world. Despite being hyper-precarious, despite being
young, despite being migrants, they have shown that
organized class power isn't a thing of the past. The
strike weapon is being transformed in the laboratory
of platform capitalism, as new management tactics and
new technologies employed by the ruling class run up
against working-class self-organization. Food-platform
workers, across national borders, are responding to

the 'future of work' with the future of class struggle. Their fight is beginning to indicate a path to renewal for the whole working-class movement, and proves that the changing composition of the working class can provide new opportunities for socialist politics, even as it demolishes old certainties. So, their experiences deserve the closest possible analysis – because that movement is the best chance we have of getting out of the mess of the twenty-first century in one piece.

In order to conduct that analysis, this book is structured as follows. First, it introduces the job, telling the story of how I started work at Deliveroo, and what an average shift was like. The next chapter analyses the technical composition of Deliveroo from the workers' point of view, with a particular focus on the system of control that governs workers. I then turn to previous examples of precarious worker resistance, looking at two historical examples (dockers and builders) to try and draw some wider lessons. Then, the next chapter moves on to the workers and their social composition. In particular, this chapter looks at the role of migration, education, housing, and culture in forming a highly diverse and militant working class. Next, I analyse the customers, and try to understand what the social role of Deliveroo is, beyond the marketing. Who uses the company, why do they use it, and what does that tell us about our society more generally? With this basis established, we reach the strikes. In this chapter, I present a first-hand account of the conflict in Brighton specifically, as well as a more general overview of the conflict across the UK and farther afield. In the second half of the chapter, I begin to focus closely on the political composition of the strikes, and how the organization of work and the city determined the tactics and organizational forms we used. The next chapter looks at the future of platforms and speculates on what could be next for companies like Deliveroo – as well as what workers could do to impose their own interests on the company. The penultimate chapter returns to strikes and looks at the most recent developments in the precarious workers' movement in the UK and farther afield.

Deliveroo is a company which combines technological developments with old-school exploitation. The way it organizes work inevitably leads to workers becoming angry, and provides them with opportunities to build embryonic solidarity. Because, despite the social diversity of the workforce and their apparent disconnection, Deliveroo workers have proved that they have the capacity to self-organize, form alliances, and fight back together. These fights have taken the form of explosions rather than patient organizing, but they have had success nonetheless. In the fire of technologically advanced and hyper-exploited capitalism, workers are forging new models of organizing and new forms of action. These aren't limited to one city or country, but have jumped from place to place, over and over again. Deliveroo workers are part of a platform workers' movement which – if it continues to develop – will end up involved in a struggle over the future of platforms themselves. The options on offer are likely to be fully automated food delivery plus mass unemployment, or platform expropriation under workers' control. The balance of power between classes will determine which will win out.

2

The Job

In the summer of 2016, I watched the London Deliveroo strike from behind a desk. At 8.15 a.m., I would cycle the 3 miles to the University of Sussex campus from Brighton, lock up my bike and sit down for another day as a policy and research assistant at the students' union. In my down time, flicking through social media, I saw friends sharing things about the strike. I saw a video, recorded on a worker's phone, of a strike convoy of hundreds of mopeds snaking through the streets, horns blaring. I watched it over and over, waiting for the day to end.

Two weeks after the Deliveroo strikes had first exploded, UberEats workers decided to follow their example and strike for better conditions. One lunch break, towards the end of the month, I went outside to call Petros Elia, the general secretary of the United Voices of the World (UVW) union. The UVW, much like the IWGB, is a small militant union which supported the strikes. We spoke for about twenty minutes, and he described how the internal dynamics of the strike movement seemed to be very unorthodox. It wasn't like standard trade unionism, there was something else going on. I wrote up our conversation in an article for *Novara Media*. I used one quote from Petros at the heart of it: 'The totally spontaneous and autonomous nature of this action is what makes it so exciting. It's not really organising as we know it – it's something else entirely. They're not following any of the strategic rules. They do what they want, and it works.'[1] This dynamism was a theme I'd soon be seeing in practice.

For the time being, however, I left the sunshine and went back to my desk with one question: why hadn't the strikes spread? I knew Deliveroo was in Brighton too, I saw mopeds with the trademark turquoise boxes passing below the windows of my flat every evening. If these conditions were national, why had they only caused a strike in London? It was impossible to tell without knowing what was actually going on in the city, and you couldn't know what was going on from the outside. Part of what made these strikes so interesting was the impenetrability of the organizing processes that generated them. Marx wrote about the way that, in capitalist society, the market, where commodities are bought and sold, is a public sphere ruled over by the ideals of Freedom, Equality and Property. But the workplace, where value is actually produced, is more like a 'hidden abode', with an entirely different set of rules.[2] That was how it felt to me, trying to understand Deliveroo: I could read all I wanted about these flexible market disruptors, but the reality of production was a mystery.

Searching for news on the strike had brought me to the attention of the algorithms. On every website I visited, I was now being served with adverts encouraging me to start working for Deliveroo. They showed me pictures of young people in colourful uniforms leaning on nice bicycles and promised me £12 an hour and total flexibility. They were inviting me into the hidden abode. Eventually, I took them up on the offer.

Getting the Job

I thought of working for Deliveroo as an experiment. It would let me understand what the work was actually like, see how I could support workers who decided to take action, and make some extra money at the same time. My students' union paycheques weren't that great, after all. I was working 8.30–5.30, but I was allowed to be flexible with my time, so if I could make up the hours elsewhere and left at 5, I reckoned I could get an evening shift in, a couple of days a week. So, in mid-September, I finally clicked on one of the ads, signed up, and got a call the same day. I arranged to do my 'trial ride' the next week.

The trial ride was not a great success. I wangled working from home so that I could be in the city at midday. We were meeting at the Level, a park in the centre of Brighton. I got there a little early and met another prospective worker. He was a student at the University of Sussex, new to the city, and looking to pick up some extra work. He reckoned starting with Deliveroo would be easier than trying to compete with the thousands of other students in the city looking for 15 hours a week at a pub or cafe. A few minutes later, the worker leading the trial showed up. He was just doing trial shifts to supplement his normal delivery work, and his role basically seemed to be to make sure we could cycle without falling off our bikes. The trial involved cycling from the Level down to a side street near the sea front. It all went okay until we got into the north Laine, an area of small streets with a complicated road system. We ended up about to ride the wrong way down a one-way street. Aware that there wasn't any time limit to complete the trial, but that you probably couldn't break the highway code and still get a job, we got off our bikes and walked part of the way there. When we got to the designated street, the trial leader demonstrated how the app functioned and gave us some advice on what hours were good to work. I was all set to start as soon as I completed some online training and picked up my kit. After the trial, I never saw either of them again.

The next step was to pick up my equipment at an 'on-boarding session'. I was expecting to be invited to an office, but instead I was told to go to a storage unit one evening next week. The unit was part of a large ware-house, run by a chain. At a guess, I'd say the other units were mostly rented by landlords and small businesses. There I met three other recruits and waited for the clos-est thing to an actual manager that I ever met. We didn't know where to go, so just stood in the small reception area, hoping we were in the right place. The almost-manager we were waiting for turned up ten minutes late, spilling out of an elevator filled to the brim with brightly coloured Deliveroo stuff. He promptly began to turn the reception into a distribution centre. He gave us a code we needed to install the app on our phone, and then began to hand out a huge load of kit: waterproof trousers and jacket, a t-shirt, a cycling jersey, a battery pack, a cheap phone mount, some even cheaper lights, a helmet, and finally the thermal backpack. For the privilege, we would have 50 per cent of our first £300 earned deducted to pay a £150 deposit. We were supposed to be able to get this back when we finished working for Deliveroo and gave the kit back. Most of the stuff he gave us would turn out to be useless, apart from the battery pack, backpack, and jacket.

Deliveroo, he explained, was split into zones, about 2.5 miles across. In some cities, you could have multiple zones, but in Brighton we just had one. The pay structure of Deliveroo varied from city to city, and for us it was a pure piece wage. We'd get £4 per delivery, with no hourly rate at all. We were told that, sometimes, when demand was high, we might get a 'surge' text, offering a variety of pay increases, ranging from an extra 50p or £1 per drop to a bonus £10 after you completed ten orders. Brighton was what was called a 'free login zone', meaning that there was no formal shift system. We could turn on the app and work at any time between 11.45 a.m. and 11 p.m. Monday to Thursday. and 9 a.m. to 11 p.m. Friday to Sunday. The almost-manager told us that we had to work a minimum of two weekends a month. I was confused – wasn't Brighton a free login zone? I thought we could work whenever we wanted? Apparently not. He said we had to work for at least two shifts of 4 hours between Friday and Sunday twice a month or we would be deactivated. This rule was never written down, but the instructions were very clear. Flexibility, it seemed, had its limits.

The three other recruits were all students, two at university and one at college. We chatted a bit about why we were starting the job. All of them had been applying for other jobs in the city but had been unsuccessful. It was a real challenge getting part-time work, particularly in September. at the start of the academic year. I'd had the same experience as a Masters student at Sussex. I ended up working a few cash-in-hand shifts on a crepe stall until the owner finally gave up on teaching me how to flip pancakes. We had a laugh about it – hopefully I would be better at delivering food. We exchanged numbers and agreed to let each other know how the job went, but then after the on-boarding I never saw any of them again either. As I was cycling home, I wondered how representative these first four recruits I'd met were: all students on bicycles, all struggling to find work, three men and one woman. I'd later find out that I was in fact joining Deliveroo at the start of a massive wave of student recruitment.

An Average Shift

I was keen to get going and do my first shift. I decided I'd start work after my day job that Thursday. I got changed, pumped up my tyres, bolted down some food, filled up a water bottle, checked my phone was fully charged, and headed out. It was later than I intended, almost 6 p.m., but no matter. I clocked on and logged in to the app, then got my first order almost immediately. It was for a pizza restaurant, five minutes away.

The labour process at Deliveroo is simple and repetitive. You open the app, log in, and select 'available for orders'. As soon as you do that, your location and availability begins to be factored into the order allocation process, and the app tells you to go to the 'zone centre'. The zone centre is a central point in the city, near the busy restaurants. Workers are told to wait there in order to make sure there is a pool of labour available and in position for when demand picks up. For us in Brighton, there were actually two zone centres, one for the cyclists at Jubilee Square and one for mopeds a few streets up at Spring Gardens, both in the north Laine area of the city. After a wait, varying in length between seconds and hours, you would get an order notification. The app would tell you which restaurant the order was for and where the restaurant was. You would then swipe 'accept' or wait two minutes for the order to auto-decline. If you accepted, as most of us did most of the time, then you'd cycle/drive to the restaurant, lock up your bike, and swipe on the app to confirm your arrival. The app would then show you the details of the order you had to collect, and a unique four-digit order code.

Then you would go inside the restaurant, tell the kitchen workers that code, and get the order – sometimes after another long wait. The restaurants were meant to call a worker on their app just before the food was ready, but some did it earlier in an attempt to reduce their delivery times. The only actual impact it had was annoying us. Some restaurants were funny about you coming in the customer entrance and wanted you to go around the back, some always made you wait for ages, some were very friendly. It often depended on whether the manager on duty was in a bad mood. If they were, you were the perfect person to take it out on – you didn't even work there, so they could be as rude as they liked. If you talked back, they could immediately report you via their version of the app.

Some couriers were very chatty with kitchen staff, and there were advantages to being nice. One evening,

I got talking with a Polish waiter whilst waiting for an order. After that, he always gave me a free Coke when I went in his restaurant. One busy Indian restaurant a few hundred metres from the zone centre had a below-ground kitchen accessed through a parking garage, and their habit of calling riders too early, plus the enclosed space, created another informal space to meet workers. One Italian restaurant forced you to wait, backpack and all, behind a door in a busy kitchen, with chefs shouting and waiters coming past at high speed. You were obviously in the way, but the managers wouldn't have you cluttering up the restaurant. When you were given the order, you were meant to check every single item was there and tap on the app to confirm. In reality, the paper bags we were given were often stapled shut, and there was no way of knowing if we were delivering the right thing or not. That part of the job was functionally impossible. Once we'd tapped all the items, we could swipe to confirm we were ready to go deliver the food.

The customer's location would then be revealed. Particularly for cyclists, this could really suck. If the customer was nearby, great: a quick £4. If the customer was farther away but the route there was flat, I could live with it. But if the customer was up a big hill, that was a real kick in the teeth. Brighton is a very hilly city, and the zone centre is almost at the bottom of a valley. Most routes involved some kind of steep incline. But seeing a route which involved any of Albion Hill, Edwards Street, Southover Street, or Elm Grove made my heart sink. Some of Brighton's roads are so steep that, back in the day, walls were built half-way down the worst culprits in order to stop runaway carts from

26

killing people. Not only did getting up these hills hurt, but each big hill you did reduced the potential length of your shift. A decent two-and-a-half-hour evening shift would involve 20-plus miles of cycling, up and down hills. If you were working at a weekend, you typically wanted to stay out for 5 or more hours – and by the point you got to 4 hours it was difficult to get up a steep road without walking. Working for Deliveroo was physically difficult.

Once you knew where you were going, you'd begin to think through the route in your head as you went through the motions of unlocking your bike and setting off. When you arrived, the app would prompt you to swipe to confirm arrival and swipe to confirm delivery. At the end of that process, you had earned £4. Now to do it again. You'd start by turning around, rolling back down whatever godforsaken hill you'd just killed yourself to get up, and go back to the zone centre. If it was busy, you might pick up another order immediately. If it was really busy, these orders tended to be from restaurants farther away. The order allocation of the app would sometimes drag you from Brighton into Hove, and keep you doing orders on one side of the zone for hours, and sometimes it'd keep sending you back and forth. But having the app tell you to cycle half-way across the zone to pick up your next order was better than waiting, unpaid, in the cold.

The story of one typical delivery in November gives you an idea of how an evening would go. It was about 6 p.m. on a weeknight. I had just arrived at the zone centre and turned on my app. There was a bench attached to the outside of a chain sushi restaurant that we all sat on when we were waiting, which we called the 'Roo bench'. I was sat there with my bike leaned up against the wall and my backpack by my feet. I was worried whether my lights were well enough charged, because I'd forgotten to plug them in during the day. I had my phone in my hand, in its waterproof case, and was chatting with a couple of the riders I knew vaguely. Then my phone buzzed, and I saw I'd got an order. I swiped to accept, told the other riders I would see them later, put my backpack on, mounted my phone on my handlebars and got on my bike. The order was for a Mexican restaurant at the bottom of London Road. The journey there would take a minute without traffic lights, or two with them. I had a choice to turn right at the top of the road and go along the main road that led up from the pier or continue straight-ish and cut through the small streets of the laines, avoiding traffic lights.

I chose the second option. Tipsy pedestrians almost got in my way going around a tight corner, but I swerved to avoid them. Then I turned left back onto the main road after the lights. The road surface here was in really bad condition and I had to weave to avoid the worst of it. Traffic was queued up to the next set of traffic lights, so I filtered through until I reached the restaurant on my left. There I faced a problem: the only locking-up spot for about 15 metres in either direction was a lamppost, which someone else was already using. There was outside seating at this restaurant, so I decided to be a bit cheeky and ask the people sitting there to make sure no one ran off with my bike whilst I went inside to pick up the food. It was a risk, but the alternative was wasting two minutes walking, locking up, walking back and then repeating the process once I'd picked up the order. I left my rear light on, and then I went inside.

The Job

I could see the flashing red light through the misted-up window, and as long as it didn't move I knew the bike was safe. I swiped on my app to say I'd arrived and gave the kitchen staff my order number. The order was for a burrito, and they never made them ahead of time at this place because they were worried about sogginess. That was fair enough, but it did mean I had to wait for five minutes whilst the chefs did a few orders for customers in the restaurant before getting around to mine. Whilst I waited, I sent a couple of messages on a group chat and checked my Twitter, keeping one eye on my flashing red light all the time. There was no space for me to sit down, so I stood awkwardly in the middle of the aisle between two small tables, acutely conscious of both being in the way of the waiting staff and looming over two couples having dinner. I always developed a paranoid fear in these situations that I would clumsily hit someone with my backpack.

Eventually, the order was ready. I put it into my thermal bag and went back outside. I got on my bike, said thanks to the customers who had kept an eye on it, and tapped and swiped to confirm everything. Then I saw the customer location. It was up Southover Street, which rises off the Level park and goes pretty much straight up to the top of the Hanover hill at a steep gradient. I had a friend who lived on an adjacent street, and he had joked with me before that he liked to watch how far Deliveroo riders could get up the road before giving up. I cut across the Level and started to climb it, getting into my lowest gear pretty much from the start. I did mean to get off and walk at some point in order to save my legs, but as I got to the first kick up in gradient, I got out the saddle and started climbing. It felt pretty easy, and I got the idea that I should just climb the whole thing out of the saddle, like some kind of Tour de France pro. It wasn't the best idea for maximizing my earnings, but it was fun. A taxi coming down the road and navigating between the cars parked on both sides passed me with barely 6 inches of room to spare. I carried on sweating my way up before turning left onto the street I was delivering to and finding the terraced house I was looking for. I leant my bike against a wall, rang the bell, handed over the food out of my backpack, wished the customer a good evening, and swiped to confirm. I didn't get another order immediately, which was a pity. I was kind of hoping it would be drop-to-drop. But anyway, I had no choice but to roll back down Southover Street, shifting my weight back as far as possible on the bike and avoiding catastrophe whilst cutting around the speed bumps. Repeat that process between four and twelve times, and you pretty much had a shift.

There were all sorts of potential disruptions and variations on this basic work sequence. The most common of these was a double or triple order. That meant that you completed deliveries to multiple customers from one restaurant and got paid £4 per drop for each. Obviously, this was a better system for us, but it really left the customer in the lurch. If you were the third person on a triple order, your food would have to spend, on average, about half an hour being bumped around in a backpack and going cold before it got to you.

If you ever had a problem, like a puncture or a crash, you could ring Deliveroo's call centre. One recurring issue was inadvertent calzone: if someone ordered a single pizza, it had a lot of space to bang about in your bag, and when climbing or descending a hill could easily get folded. You'd arrive and take the box out your back-pack, only to find tomato sauce soaking through the cardboard. The call centre workers responded to this by reordering the pizza (at the company's expense) and telling you to offer the pizza to the customer. Sometimes, however, the call centre workers would tell you to give it to the homeless. I suspected that some call centre workers were going off script in an effort to help people out, or maybe the company just changed its tune in order to get some good publicity. Either way, I didn't struggle to find a homeless person to give it to. During almost every shift I worked in April, I passed a homeless encampment by St Peter's church. About ten people were living there in tents and shanties. There was a banner hung from the trees: 'This Land is Ours!' But by the end of the month, the camp had been cleared to make way for a temporary theatre venue.

All sorts of weird stuff could happen during a shift. One Saturday night, I was going down to the seafront to pick up some fish and chips, when a young guy, about 18 years old, leaned out the passenger window of a silver van that was driving slightly ahead of me. He looked straight at me and shouted: 'your mum's a fucking c***!' People think they can be rude to delivery workers just because you've got a big thermal backpack on. I really didn't like it when they did that, so I shouted straight back – '*your* mum's a fucking c***!' We went back and forth a few times, then he got the driver of the van to change lanes, pull in front of me and slow right down. I overtook and went ahead to the traffic lights, about 10 metres farther on.

Now, these traffic lights are at a junction right in the centre of town, slap-bang between Brighton's two most famous landmarks, the pavilion and the pier. The city's central police station is about a minute's drive away, and there is CCTV everywhere. I thought the whole thing was over.

Then I heard the passenger door slam shut. The passenger walked up behind me and started shouting again. 'What did you say about my mum?' At this point I started to get a bit worried. He was clearly acting out. But I was angry, so I didn't do the sensible thing and de-escalate. Why should he have the right to scream in my face for no reason? So, rather than pointing out that he had started the whole mum thing, I just repeated what I'd said. He threatened to break the bottle of cider he was drinking in my face. I called him a weirdo and, as I went to ride off, he tried to push me in front of a taxi. Fortunately, the driver saw it coming and slammed on his brakes. I just about stayed upright and cycled away, shaken. The lack of respect paid to delivery workers meant that people felt they could have a go at you without any consequences. On top of that, we were often working in the drinking hubs of the city on Friday and Saturday nights, on our own. It was a dangerous combination.

There were certain performance standards we were meant to reach during our shifts. Apparently, we were meant to accept 90 per cent of orders and deliver them within a certain time. I say 'apparently', because for some reason I never got the 'service level assessment' emails which gave me the stats on how fast I was delivering and what percentage of orders I accepted. Other workers got irregular updates on their position relative to the average, minimum and target speeds and rates. Failing to meet these standards could lead to your 'supplier agreement' contract being terminated immediately. Experienced workers sometimes refused orders during busy periods if the restaurant was too far away, in order to try and maximize their hourly wage, but that rarely amounted to 10 per cent of total orders. For slower riders, these emails could be a constant source of anxiety. We were all under time pressure, and it was hard to forget it.

Payment could be inaccurate and/or late; Deliveroo would sometimes pay riders for fewer orders than they had actually completed and would often do so a day or two after we were meant to be paid. Because, as 'independent contractors', we weren't on PAYE, payday wasn't set in stone any more. Instead of a payday, we had 'fee payments' which were received at the end of a 'fee cycle', just as if we were private companies. Only we didn't have the cash flow of small businesses, we had the cash flow of employees. The two didn't match. So, some workers would have to email and call to correct and chase up on payments in order to guarantee they could pay rent and put food on the table.

Over my time at Deliveroo, I got used to getting surge texts. What I hadn't fully understood when we were first introduced to surges during the on-boarding was that they were a fairly frequently used way for management to alter the piece rate in order to increase the labour available to the platform at short notice. Because there was no formal shift system, Deliveroo had to use payment incentives. Whenever you got the text, you'd immediately check the weather. Usually you'd make a calculation: was the weather *that* bad? I knew riders who didn't make that calculation, though. If it was a boost, they were working, end of.

The boosts had another strange effect. This meant we knew that a higher piece rate was possible – if they could afford to pay us £5 a drop during peak times, there was no clear reason to reduce it to £4 during less busy times, when we would be doing fewer deliveries per hour. But we also knew that labour undersupply was forcing Deliveroo to increase wages, and that it might not last for ever.

In late 2016, just after I started, these surges were quite common. Probably a third of the shifts I did over that period were partly or fully covered by surge delivery rates. As a result, my wages were pretty high: I was going from drop to drop, never going back to the zone centre, always busy. I was earning an average of something like £12 an hour, before costs. But Deliveroo had already begun a strategy to reduce their labour costs and cover peak times without paying premium rates. This strategy was simple and brutal. In order to increase the number of riders available, they would recruit large numbers of students. The resulting labour oversupply didn't hurt them: if there were 300 orders to be done in an hour, they paid 300 x £4 in labour, regardless of whether those orders were done by 100 workers or 300 workers. In fact, if there was a large pool of available labour, their delivery times went down, because there were workers always ready for a new order, thereby improving their customer service. But, for the workers, that was the difference between £12 an hour and £4 an hour. In late 2016, new workers were starting every day. I was one of them, but for at least two months after I started work more and more people were signed up. This strategy, and the changes it produced, would eventually lead to the first overt conflict in Brighton between workers and management.

During my first few shifts, I wanted to speak to other workers whenever I could. Because those early shifts were so busy, this mostly meant having quick chats in restaurant kitchens. These passing interactions were often not much more than exchanging names and a smile. Everyone was going drop-to-drop and wanted to make the most of it. When I was out on the road, I made an effort to smile and wave at other workers at traffic lights or when I passed them, and 90 per cent of the time they'd do the same. Over time, I found that midweek evening shifts were easier for me to fit into my life, even if they weren't always so busy. On these shifts, whenever the pace of work slowed down, a group of us would start assembling at the zone centre. At first, we talked about bikes – about chains, brakes, pedals, tyres, and gears. It was the one thing absolutely everyone at the cyclist zone centre had in common. Some people were bigger bike nerds than others, and they tended to dish out advice to those of us with less of a clue. Somebody helped me align my back brakes so that the brake blocks lasted longer, and I helped somebody else tighten their cables.

We weren't the kind of couriers who wore odd-shaped cycling caps and rode fixed gear bikes. All the previous examples of successful organizing I knew of, such as the IWGB courier branch, or those who organized with the Industrial Workers of the World (IWW) in Chicago in the early 2000s, had relied on a subcultural courier community to create a sense of solidarity.[3] Workers knew each other because they had all participated in these mad cross-city courier races, gone to the same pubs, used the same bike shops, and been part of a common social scene. But that wasn't the case for us. We were an undifferentiated mass of deskilled labour. Small groups of workers did have things in common, but it was rare you found something apart from bikes and working conditions you could all chat about. Trade unionists involved in the original London dispute told me that the groups which had started the strike there met outside of work in one of two places: either Gabber raves or Friday prayers. Gabber is a genre of dance music, originating in the working-class neighbourhoods around the container port of Rotterdam in the Netherlands in the 1990s. Describing it as 'aggressive' is an understatement. It's at least 180 beats per minute, and most people find that in order to enjoy it you need to consume large amounts of drugs. Not really the same vibe as Friday prayers at East London Mosque.

Gradually, over the course of a couple of shifts, I moved on to talking about work with the faces I recognized. I heard about why they were working for Deliveroo: the father who was working sixty-hour weeks, no matter how low his hourly rate went, because he was earning more than he would on Jobseekers allowance and he had to support his baby boy. The migrant worker who couldn't find other work because his English wasn't good enough. The musician who was struggling to make a living on bar work alone. The student whose loan wouldn't cover his rent, let alone his food bills. The graduate who couldn't stand the manager in his old low-skill low-paid job. The 17-year-old who cycled 4 miles to Brighton before he even started his shift because he needed to be bringing in extra money and the Education Maintenance Allowance (a £30-a-week subsidy for college students from low-income families) had been cut during the first round of austerity in 2010. They were all keen to talk about why they did the job, how long they'd be doing it for, what they liked, and what they didn't.

Some had been working at Deliveroo since it started in Brighton. Back then, it had been an hourly rate of £7 plus £1 per delivery and relied on a more formal scheduling system. One worker told me about how the order volume was so low that he used to get himself put on the quiet midweek afternoon shifts and switch on his app whilst lying on his sofa watching TV. It wasn't like that anymore. The switch from an hourly rate with a per-drop bonus to a pure piece rate had infuriated everyone. Apparently, at the time, there had been some discussion of going on strike or joining a union, particularly when the workers saw what happened in London. But nothing had come of it, and as Deliveroo had refined their process, the cushy sofa-job had disappeared. The transition from hourly wage to piece rate had led to a serious increase in the amount of work you had to do.

After a couple of months spent just talking to as many workers as possible, I began to understand that Deliveroo workers were already well organized. Stupidly, I'd bought the myth and believed we would be totally disconnected from each other, just atomized individuals scattered across the city. Even though the London strike had been evidence to the contrary, it hadn't sunk in. Now, however, I was coming to understand how wrong I was. Deliveroo workers had well-established channels for communication and organization already on the go below the surface. In person, these channels were the two zone centres. Groups of mopeds and cyclists knew each other well and would meet up there when it went quiet. The online channels were various WhatsApp and Facebook groups which had been set up well over a year ago by long-term Deliveroo workers in the city. Following a few conversations in person at the zone centre, I got added to them. The group chats consisted of workers from Brighton talking on a daily basis about their working conditions, whether it was busy or not, helping each other navigate Deliveroo's online processes, keeping track of when payday was, organizing five-a-side football games, giving advice on how to register as self-employed and work out their expenses/taxes, and cracking jokes. These networks were completely hidden to everyone but the workers, but they played an important social function. If you needed an Allen key, they could fulfil a very practical function too. Sometimes, however, that practical function was altogether more serious.

In early 2017, a rider started messaging the chat. He was sitting by the side of the road, confused. He felt sick, his heart was racing, and he'd started to experience severe abdominal pain. He'd been working all day, and now he just couldn't go any farther. It was immediately clear something was badly wrong. Other riders started messaging him, asking whether he was okay, trying to help. Someone told him to share his location. A couple of workers cancelled the orders they were doing and headed straight for him. When they arrived, they realized he was freezing cold. He had been working for hours in sub-zero temperatures with only a couple of layers of cheap cotton clothes under his jacket. At the start of his shift he'd sweated a lot, soaked his clothes, and then become increasingly cold. They flagged down a taxi, paid for it to take him to hospital, and locked his bike up. Later, the rider messaged the chat again. He said thank you for the help. At the hospital, they'd said he was experiencing the first stages of hypothermia. The group chat had managed to get him help in a few minutes.

Sometimes these group chats had to function as a self-defence mechanism for workers. For moped riders, bike theft was a real risk. For cyclists, it tended to be mugging that was the biggest worry. Either way, chats became a way to warn about recent hotspots and potential threats. In Brighton, the situation got so bad that some moped riders started carrying improvised weapons in case anyone tried to jump them. I knew one worker who had a hammer with him at all times. At first, I just assumed he was being irrational – if someone was so determined to nick your moped that you had to defend yourself with a hammer, surely you should let it go? After all, losing a bike was better than getting stabbed. One evening, at the moped zone centre, I probed for more details. 'If I lose the bike, I lose everything', he said. The bike was on a hire-purchase agreement: if it was stolen, he'd lose the ability to work but still have monthly instalments to pay. Workers knew they couldn't rely on the police. If they called to say a bike was getting nicked, a patrol car wouldn't turn up for twenty minutes, if it turned up at all – by which time the bike was long gone. In most cases, once a bike was stolen, there was no chance of recovering it.

In summer 2017, London workers became the victims of a series of acid attacks. This brought home the grim reality that it wasn't just the bikes at risk. Workers in London started refusing to work in certain zones after 8 p.m. At traffic lights, they kept their head on a swivel, watching for threats. In July, they organized a demonstration against acid attacks. Hundreds went to Parliament Square to demand safer working conditions. But they didn't just demonstrate. Some riders took more direct action. Bike thieves weren't given an easy time. Riders wouldn't always call the police if they saw someone trying to get at another worker's bike. Sometimes they'd go after the thief themselves. I have seen video footage of five workers steaming out of a restaurant into a wannabe bike thief and kicking him up and down a London high street. These workers trusted each other implicitly when faced with a threat. Similarly, whenever an immigration raid was going down, workers would rapidly forward messages from group to group to prevent workers with questionable status getting caught up in it. The memory of the Byron Burger deportations went deep.

Over time, I gradually became integrated into the Deliveroo community. I would check the WhatsApp groups once a day at least, and when I waited at the zone centre there would usually be a few workers I knew. When I started the job, I'd felt alone. As I was charging around the city at night, stressed to the eyeballs, that isolation was pretty unpleasant. I had been hyper-aware that something could go wrong very easily, and that I wouldn't have any support if it did. But now I was starting to feel part of a community, one which could help me out if needs be. I'd found out that there was a significant underlying solidarity linking together a large portion of the workforce on a daily basis. It was this solidarity which we'd later rely on.

3

The System of Control

When a boss buys a workers' labour-power, they are buying a potential to work for a certain amount of time. However, that potential won't always actually be fulfilled. Workers tend to find ways to take it easy. Unlike machines or raw materials, workers have a capacity to resist. This resistance can take a more or less organized form. It could mean hiding in a store cupboard for fifteen minutes to go on your phone, or it could mean a strike. So, for a boss, the problem of labour-power is that it is *indeterminate*. Paying a wage buys them the potential for work to get done and value to be produced, but they have to develop a 'system of control' in order to turn that variable potential into a reality.[1] This system of control has two parts. First, it needs to coordinate the overall labour process as efficiently as possible. Second, it needs to discipline workers to make sure their indeterminate labour-power is being applied to this labour process as intensively as possible.

Management is primarily the science of that system of control. It is interested in breaking workers' resistance in order to produce the most value possible from a given sum of labour-power. Right from its origins, in Fredrick Taylor's writing on 'scientific management' in the early twentieth century, management theory reflects the obsession of capitalist managers with the question of how to force workers to work harder for longer in order to produce more. For Taylor, the main problem facing bosses was 'soldering' – otherwise known as workers going slow. He believed, quite rightly, that most workers keep something back from their boss. They don't wring every last drop of effort out of themselves every shift. He wanted to develop a system whereby managers would be able to intensify work. In order to do so, managers needed to understand the labour process at least as well as the workers who currently dominated it. Taylor's thesis was that, by making management more scientific, its effectiveness could be improved.[2] Harry Braverman, a Marxist intellectual, identified Taylor's system of scientific management as having two processes at its core: 'work intensification' and 'deskilling'[3] – that is to say, making workers work harder, and reducing workers' control over their own work. These two processes remain the fundamental strategies of capitalist management today.

So, when we are discussing a job, we're also discussing a specific conflict. It's a conflict between the strategies of resistance developed by the workers and the system of control developed by the boss. Like in an arms race, the methods adopted by one side are reacted to by the other, leading to a constant escalating development as both sides attempt to get the upper hand. This back and forth between workers and bosses is the basis of capitalist development. It's the motor that forces forward the creation of new technology, the reorganization of work, the growth of new markets, the change of state services and the rest, because the workplace is the only source of profit on which the whole system relies. Even inter-capitalist competition is premised on which company can most effectively use labour-power to produce value, and if one company is losing the fight against its workers' resistance, it's doomed to fail. The fight over indeterminate labour-power defines the shape of the labour process, but also the shape of wider capitalist society.

At Deliveroo, the system of control is characterized by some specific technological developments. It's important to understand these developments first, so that we can understand the way in which workers reacted with their own strategic resistance. So, the rest of this chapter focuses on explaining and analysing the ways in which indeterminate labour-power is managed by Deliveroo's system of control in order to intensify work, deskill labour, and cut costs.

Algorithmic Management

One thing was obvious to me, as soon as I started working for Deliveroo: it was great not having a supervisor. There was no one breathing down my neck, telling me to go faster, do this, do that. When I'd worked in a hotel kitchen, I couldn't lounge about. Even if there was nothing to do, I had to look busy by pretending to polish glasses. Human supervision was one of the worst parts of the labour-process. I wasn't alone in that experience. That inter-personal relationship between worker and supervisor is often one of the most fraught in any workplace. They're the person who makes your life harder, every day; the person who stops you taking extra-long breaks, changes around your shifts, tells you to be more productive, makes you fill in some bureaucratic form, and so on. At Deliveroo, I felt free of that.

In the classical form of courier work, a dispatcher supervises workers over a radio. They check where workers are, when they've completed a job, and distribute new jobs. They are a key element of the system of control which manages indeterminate labour-power. However, they also have a second role. They coordinate the labour process. From a centralized point, they make sure that things are picked up and dropped off at the right place at the right time. When Marx was describing the importance of control and management in capitalist work processes, he used the example of war: 'that a capitalist should command on the field of production, is now as indispensable as that a general should command on the field of battle'.[4] To apply Marx's idea to classical courier work, the dispatcher plays the role of a sergeant: they are a worker whose job is to maintain control of other workers and translate the orders of the general into the actions of the soldiers. They occupy an intermediate class position. That is to say, their job is to serve the interests of the bosses above all else, despite not actually being bosses themselves. In return, they get premium wages and conditions. The dispatcher plays a key role in implementing the whole system of control.

At Deliveroo, the labour process is actually pretty similar to other kinds of courier work. The key difference is in the chain of command, as a result of 'algorithmic management'.[5] Under algorithmic management, the role of the dispatcher is transformed. In practice, algorithmic management is the partial automation of supervision and labour process coordination through the use of information technology. The highest level of manager left in a city is a 'driver lead', an almost-manager, who is relegated to acting as a problem-solver. The majority of the work performed by a dispatcher is now automated as a function of the app.

In 2017, Rohan Pradhan, Deliveroo's director of strategic projects, revealed what Deliveroo management call their 'real-time dispatch algorithm': Frank. When an order is received, Frank takes two seconds to estimate preparation/delivery time and assign a delivery worker who 'has the best characteristics to fulfil that specific order based on distance, type of location and other factors'.[6] Assuming Deliveroo has a symmetrical back-office process to other food platforms, the human role in this process is reduced to supervising Frank as it goes about its work. The workers who do this are basically 'app watchers' sitting behind screens in a centralized office, from which they supervise the function of the algorithmic system. Grasping the implications of this kind of automation is vital for understanding the reality of work and the strategies of worker resistance which emerged at Deliveroo.

But first, it's important to understand why capitalist companies invest in technology at all. Capitalism is fundamentally a system based on producing more and more of the capitalist form of value (usually expressed in terms of money). However, it's not a unified process: different individual companies all compete via markets to produce the most value. Investment in technology is one way for one company to gain an advantage over another. Technology does this by increasing the productivity of labour-power. A company can produce more relative surplus value, which will eventually be converted into profits, if it has more productive technology than its competitors. This productive advantage forces other competitors to invest in the same technology, gradually reducing to zero the relative surplus value advantage gained by the company which invested first as the new technology becomes standard.

So, there is no incentive for a capitalist company to invest in technology unless it results in a competitive advantage. Take the example of car washes. In the UK, the technology exists for car washes to be highly automated. The ones you see attached to garages rarely need much human supervision. But, by exploiting migrant workers with complicated legal status, bosses acting as gangmasters can undercut the costs of automated car washes and outcompete garages. If there was a natural tendency towards technological development inherent in capitalism, no car wash would work this way. Any rational person can see that it's a waste of human potential to force people to complete menial and unnecessary tasks. But capitalism has no such inherent tendency. In fact, under capitalism, it is profit and competition which dictate what work gets automated, not human need. Car washes could be automated – but hyper-exploited labour is just so cheap.[7]

As a result, the technology developed under capitalism isn't neutral. It emerges in specific social and economic contexts to serve the interests of a specific class of people. Historian of technology David F. Noble proved this point with reference to a cycle of technological development in the US after World War Two.[8] The US Air Force needed new fighter planes based on the latest technology. These planes needed to have their parts manufactured to a very high level of accuracy, and the supply needed to be absolutely constant – with no hiccups due to the variability of human labour. The metal industry began to investigate how to pursue programmable automation of machine tools to meet these standards. One initial option was 'record-playback'. Record-playback was a very simple programming method that essentially allowed machinists working with machine tools to do the mechanical equivalent of copy and paste. All the skilled worker had to do was produce a metal part manually once, and then the programmed machine tool could repeat that process over and over again. By concentrating the control of production in the hands of the shop floor machinist, it functioned as a 'skill multiplier'.

Numerical control was another similar programming mechanism, but with totally different skill mechanics. Engineers of numerical control called it an 'automatic machinist'. Under numerical control, a machinist produced the part manually once, and information on that action was recorded. A different worker, artificially separated from the shop floor, would convert the information collected from the action of the machinist into a blueprint program for the machine via a process of calculation. These 'part programmers' would have as their sole job the conversion of shop-floor information into generic blueprints, a task that required quite limited skill. Another worker, often a woman on half the pay of the part programmer and the machinist, then typed up these blueprints in machine-readable form on paper tape using a coding machine. This tape was then sent to the shop floor and fed into the machine tool by the machinist, who then supervised its operation. The cooperation of these three workers eliminated the need for a skilled machinist, reducing the power of workers in the process. As Noble puts it: 'whereas record-playback was a reproducer and, thus, a multiplier of skill, extending the reach of the machinist, numerical control was an abstract synthesizer of skill, circumventing and eliminating altogether the need for the machinist'.[9] This cooperation was also now taking place across three different workplaces rather than on one factory floor. As the division of labour increases, so does the cooperation necessary to make the whole process function – but that cooperation becomes increasingly difficult to understand.

The period between the mid-1950s and the mid-1960s saw numerical control emerge as the dominant technology. This was no objective process of technological superiority. Numerical control was, for shop-floor workers, clearly the inferior technology. It necessitated a whole bureaucracy of office workers and took all of the interesting bits of out of the job of the machinist. But this process of technological development expressed the social power relations of the society in which the choice between numerical control and record-playback was made. Ultimately, the choice between the two was down to the bosses – and they didn't much care what machinists thought about it. In the first instance, numerical control was preferred by the US Air Force because of its elimination of 'human error'. Later, as Harry Braverman argued, it became preferred across manufacturing because of the potential it offered to deskill and disempower the shop-floor machinist. Once deprived of skill, machinists could then be forced to work faster and faster. The machines themselves could have an inbuilt, programmed speed of work that could not be slowed down by tired operatives. As Noble argues, 'Machinists in the job shop would now become mere machine tenders like their brothers and sisters on the assembly line, disciplined by foremen but by machines as well.'[10] Throughout this process, the needs and desires of human workers were disregarded in favour of a constant drive for relative surplus value production. Braverman, who worked in the metal industry, described how, 'powered by the needs of the capital accumulation process, [technological development] becomes a frenzied drive which approaches the level of a generalised social insanity'.[11] This insanity, of course, is not so illogical when considered from the standpoint of the factory owner and their shareholder mates.

Deliveroo's automation of management fits this same general pattern of technological development for the good of bosses not workers, despite the dramatically different circumstances. Algorithmic management, like a system of deskilled factory labour, is designed to further the exploitation of labour-power to provide a competitive advantage to the bosses who invest in it.

There are four specific aspects of the competitive advantage gained via Deliveroo's system of algorithmic management. First, it increases the possible complexity of labour process coordination at lower cost. Algorithms are better at multi-factor calculation and planning of the labour process than human dispatchers, and, given the adaptive potential introduced by machine learning, they can get better at it over time. Second, it increases the amount of data that can be collected from the labour process. Human dispatchers retain

49

information and develop specialized knowledge, but no person's brain could store the quantity of data generated by the Deliveroo app. Third, it gets rid of the most obvious source of human error. Human dispatchers make frequent small mistakes. On top of that, they often develop favourite riders who they give preferential treatment to. This process of favouritism clearly functions as a disciplinary mechanism, so has potential uses for management, but it also causes inefficiencies. With algorithmic management, a manger can eliminate error and implement a more efficient system of favouritism and victimization. Fourth, algorithmic management can be replicated in lots of new locations for little or no additional cost. The function of the app can be supervised from a central, continental office rather than local dispatch offices. As a result, Deliveroo is very light on its feet. Expansion needn't involve recruiting reliable and experienced dispatchers on full-time contracts and organized into shifts – the algorithm is always ready to go. Combined, these key advantages have been at the heart of why Deliveroo has been able to expand so fast.

All this automation might seem, from the capitalist point of view, to be an unqualified advantage. But human supervisors have two functions. As well as maximizing the efficiency of the labour process and coordinating workers' efforts, they discipline workers. They make sure that workers put their back into it, don't skive, and don't cut corners. When you pay workers an hourly wage, the system of control a boss uses has to involve constant supervision by someone who can make sure every minute of that hour is being used for profit. But when Deliveroo had paid an hourly wage with a bonus per drop, lots of workers had taken the mickey. They were taking advantage of the fact that Deliveroo's system of control was built on a fundamental flaw: it automated management, but the algorithm was only able to do part of the job. It could coordinate the labour process with incredible accuracy and ability, but it couldn't discipline workers. The app watcher who supervises the app in a centralized office has no real-time feed of information beyond location – they don't know the couriers and they don't know the city. Between the two, the job of enforcing work intensification, one of the key parts of a system of control, had fallen through the cracks. As a result, individual strategies of resistance like skiving were simple to pull off. Frank, the algorithm, wasn't a very strict supervisor. They had a problem.

Work Intensification

Deliveroo needed to fill the gaps in their strategy of control. More specifically, they needed an answer to the question of work intensification. When order volume wasn't guaranteed and they were just starting out in the city, they needed to offer an hourly wage to make sure workers were consistently available. But, over time, business picked up. By the time I started, they had a big pool of labour and a lot of orders, and as a result they had switched to a per-drop piece wage. This change in the payment structure forced workers to either go faster or earn less.

Piece rates are not a new way of intensifying work. They were integral to the development of the original sweated labour system in the textile industry in the UK, from which we get the term 'sweatshops'. As Marx put it: 'given piece-wage, it is naturally the personal interest of the labourer to strain his labour-power as intensely as possible; this enables the capitalist to raise more easily the normal degree of intensity of labour'. As a result, Marx said it was: 'the form of wages most in harmony with the capitalist mode of production'.[12] Piece wages were just as integral to the development of capitalism in the US, where the spread of piece wages was a key part of intensifying factory labour in the late nineteenth century. In 1885, the Connecticut Bureau of Labour Statistics called the piece wage a 'moral force which corresponds to machinery as a physical force'.[13] The reason for this centrality in both the UK and US is that piece wages force you to take on the job of managing your own productivity.

If a Deliveroo worker in a piece wage zone starts a shift with one delivery in one hour, they need to do an hour with three deliveries in order to bring their hourly average up to £8. That means that you had to wring every possible delivery you could out of the peak times, going from drop to drop without a pause for as long as you could, because you never knew when order volume might drop off, and you would end up relying on a £12 hour to supplement a £4 hour. As a result, the work process became increasingly sped up. The intensification problem of algorithmic management was being solved through a piece wage structure.

As well as speeding up the work process, a piece wage also went some way towards undermining embryonic solidarity between workers, because we were all competing for orders. In an assembly-line situation, the rates paid per piece have historically been a point of collective action. By negotiating on-the-job pay increases via wildcat strikes and slowdowns, car manufacturing workers across the world have, time and time again, been able to win big concessions.[14] In the 1970s, Tony Cliff argued that, although piece wages had once been 'a very effective method of intensive exploitation', that was changing: 'In highly organised plants, workers can gain from it [piece wages] higher wages and a degree of control over the organisation of the plant.'[15] Henry Ford foresaw the possibility of collective struggle over the rate per piece in factory environments, and that threat was part of what induced him to introduce his idea of the 5-dollar day. He was willing to pay a much higher wage if it avoided the problems of bargaining on the job.[16]

But when piece wages aren't collective, and the stages of the labour process don't rely on the cooperation between one worker and another, they can have the opposite effect. At Deliveroo, piece wages induced an environment where we were all competing for orders. You could be as friendly as you liked, but sometimes it was impossible to ignore that some couriers sat on the other side of the square at the zone centre, away from the rest of us. They thought that, by being 10 metres closer to some restaurants, they would get more orders. Maybe it worked, maybe it didn't, but the sense that we were all in this together suffered as a result. Some riders really felt the pressure and used to harass workers in restaurants when their order was slow in coming out the kitchen. They knew it wasn't on, and other couriers told them so, but that was what the pressure of the piece wage did to people.

Self-intensification was an odd experience. In my day job at the students' union, I'd become quite talented at taking unsupervised breaks. When I went to the pub with my mate who worked nights in a supermarket, we'd swap stories about the inventive methods we used to skive off at work. But all that commitment to taking my time went down the tubes when I turned on the app. The first thing that made me think like my own boss was the process of finding a restaurant, fiddling with my lights, locking up my bike, finding the right entrance, waiting for my order, packing it in the thermal bag, going outside again, unlocking my bike, and getting going. It took far longer than I anticipated. Without practice, the whole routine could take over five minutes, assuming there wasn't a long wait for the order (which there frequently was). If I was just paid an hourly wage, I'd have taken a leisurely approach to the whole process. But as I needed to be as fast as possible, I began to find ways to cut the whole routine down to one or two minutes. After that, I began to memorize every shortcut I could across the city, and convenient places to lock up near popular restaurants. I was becoming a very effective supervisor.

Work intensification is a general feature of work under capitalism. But work intensification when you work on the road means something quite specific: a continual pressure to increase the risks you take. The piece wage system encourages you to take chances on every shift. If you're less careful, you make more money. Over time, you become desensitized to danger which, in another context, would make you slam on the brakes and stop weaving through traffic. It wouldn't have taken much for something to go wrong – just a pedestrian to step out into the road, or for me not to notice that a bus was turning left, and I could have been in serious danger.

But because I was too busy thinking about getting my average hourly rate over minimum wage after costs, I didn't make safe decisions.

We would sometimes hear on the WhatsApp groups that someone had crashed and hurt themselves. Riders broke bones dodging potholes and going down in icy conditions. When a gale was coming off the sea your backpack could act as a sail, and you'd get blown across the road, out of control, into the other lane. No workers died on the job in Brighton, that we knew of. But every time an ambulance whizzed past, you knew there was a possibility that something had gone horribly wrong. I'd heard of one rider who came off his moped at speed, shattered his kneecap and had been off work (unpaid) for five months. As I'd seen first-hand, the requirements for becoming a Deliveroo rider were hardly stringent. There was no guarantee that every worker had the technical skill to get themselves out of trouble. And whenever the weather got really bad: 'Surge. Earn £6.00 a drop tonight. Ride safe!'

Self-imposed work intensification meant that, for the first time in my life, I started getting into arguments with other road users. After a few months of work, I had learnt the patterns of the traffic lights at major junctions. By remembering when they changed, you could get out of the junction five to ten seconds quicker. One midweek evening shift in January, I was desperate for orders. I'd been at the zone centre for twenty minutes before I got a pizza order from the seafront to take up the steep, long hill to Queens Park in East Brighton. On the way back to the zone centre, I was assigned another order for a noodle bar. Things were finally getting busy, and I needed to make the most of it. It was bitterly cold, and my hands were struggling to grip the bars, so I didn't want to be out for long. I pulled out of the lights at the bottom of the hill where Edwards Street meets the Old Steine a few seconds early, trying to make good time across the city, when I heard a shout behind me. There was another cyclist, gesturing. I couldn't make out what he was on about. I changed up to my big chainring and stepped on the pedals. As I pulled up at a junction a couple of hundred metres farther on, the cyclist caught up with me.

He was a middle-aged man, out of breath and pissed off. Really pissed off. He started shouting about how Deliveroo was making all the cyclists in the city less safe. He thought the risk I'd taken in pulling off early meant that people wouldn't respect cyclists, and so put him in danger. I didn't have time to think about it, I just exploded. I was shouting right back, asking if he'd pay me to go slower. Another Deliveroo worker, a moped, pulled over to make sure everything was alright. I broke the conversation off and pulled out from the junction, shaking with anger. On reflection, he was probably right. We all knew that we rode in unsafe ways in order to shave a few seconds off our journey times, and it probably was bad for cyclists and the city as a whole to have a load of stressed-out workers bombing down hills, cutting through traffic, jumping lights, and swerving pedestrians. But what could we do about it? When I commuted to my full-time job, there was no way I'd take the risks I took when I was working for Deliveroo. But when I had to make as many deliveries an hour as possible in order to make a decent wage, I felt like I had to do what I had to do. It was just part of the job.

And that was the thing – it was, deliberately, by

design, just part of the job. Because the riskier your job is, the more Deliveroo benefits. They have no responsibility to replace a broken bike and no responsibility to pay you wages whilst you lie in bed with a broken leg. But if you take risk after risk just to get a better average wage, they do get the advantages of faster deliveries and better service. The worker takes all the risk, and Deliveroo get all the reward. University College London (UCL) researchers have identified that platform workers on pay-per-drop wages face significant health and safety problems. In their survey, 40 per cent of respondents reported having been in a crash severe enough to damage their bike/car/moped. In their words: 'These faceless digital brokers [platforms] take no responsibility for the health and safety of the people who accrue income for them.' Their recommendation is that piece wages be abolished and replaced by decent hourly wages.[17] As time goes on, it becomes increasingly clear that the collective interests of platform workers and bosses are fundamentally opposed on the questions of work intensification and safety.

In May 2018, I heard of the death of a food-platform worker in Philadelphia. Pablo Avendano worked for Caviar, a platform with an almost identical model to Deliveroo. He was hit from behind by an SUV whilst crossing a junction during a torrential downpour. In the words of his friends, Pablo's death was: 'a tragedy that can be laid at the feet of a capitalist system that squeezes us for everything we've got'.[18] A few days later, a 28-year-old JustEat courier in Milan lost a leg after going under a tram. The systems of control built into the labour process of food-delivery platforms force workers to take more and more risks in order to earn a decent wage, and, in some cases, work intensification can be fatal.

Talking about the invention of the factory, Marx wrote how 'with the regularity of the seasons, [the factory] issues its list of the killed and wounded in the industrial battle'.[19] Today, we could say the same of the app – only now no comprehensive list of victims is kept. These tragedies were not the first and, unless something changes, they will not be the last.

Black Box

Throughout all the risks of the labour process, a Deliveroo worker is constantly checking their app. It is the interface that controls their every move. But, despite this reliance on the app, workers are left in the dark about how it works.

You know roughly what inputs go into the app (customer orders, worker location and status, restaurant preparation) and understand the outputs in the form of instructions, but you have no idea about the exact calculations and processes that turn one into the other. This is an example of a 'black box' system.[20] The app is understood by workers in terms of its inputs and outputs, without having a clue about its internal operations.

But we didn't just accept that the app was a black box and give up. Workers have an instinctive drive to understand how their workplace is organized. Maurice Glaberman, a US car plant worker in the 1950s, described how he and his workmates were always trying to get away from their machines in order to wander around the factory and see the whole system at work.[21]

That impulse to understand the productive process, undergirded by the desire to control it, wasn't alien to Deliveroo workers. Speculation about how the app worked was rife. Elaborate theories were developed at the zone centre. One popular one was that our location is scanned every five seconds, and the person closest to the restaurant during the five seconds when the restaurant calls the rider gets the order. But these theories were a combination of guesswork and rumour, concocted before we had even the few details released about 'Frank' by Rohan Pradhan. The knowledge of how our work was coordinated was hidden from us.

This ignorance was combined with total reliance upon the app. Because we had no independent ability to coordinate the labour process or do things our own way, we had to follow instructions to the letter. At the same time, automated management can't make concessions to workers about how work is organized, or make any of the usual compromises you'd expect from a human supervisor. There is no capacity for flexibility built into the system from either direction.

As a result, algorithmic management is authoritarian management. The app spits out a sequence of repetitive commands, and you just have to do it. There was something quite brutal about the simplification of the labour process and what it did to the way you felt about work. Charlie Chaplin's 1936 film *Modern Times* shows the way in which work on an assembly line messed with workers' heads and bodies, trapping them into the constant repetition of one specialized process. In Ford manufacturing plants during the period, this level of specialization reached astonishing levels. For example, it was one worker's job to 'ream and bush the T 225 for stub axle arm left T 270' a full 850 times in an eight-hour day.[22] Workers' response to this mind-numbing repetition was often just to not turn up to work. Daily rates of unauthorized absence at Ford in 1913 ran at 10 per cent, and annual labour turnover was at 370 per cent. Ford had to employ 52,000 workers throughout the year to keep a constant workforce of 13,600 at any one time.[23] If you wanted to make a similar film about Deliveroo, it would probably focus on the way in which couriers submit totally to the orders of an impersonal system. You just kept swiping to accept, swiping to accept, 850 times a day.

The black box disempowered you not only by being totally uncompromising, but also by creating an information hierarchy. When we headed to a restaurant to pick up an order, we had no idea where that order would end up being delivered. Information about the delivery process was only revealed to us stage by stage, to stop us calling up and getting unassigned from orders which were particularly difficult or long. But, whilst we could barely work out what we'd be doing in five minutes' time, the algorithm had a constant stream of incredibly precise location and speed data which could be processed alongside order data and all sorts of other metrics to manage our work. Machine learning processes could make decisions based on all this information, and those decisions could change how much money we earned. But we never knew if, when or how those decisions were being made. The human watching the app in Deliveroo HQ also presumably played some kind of role, but we had no idea about the specifics.

When Taylor first laid out the goal of scientific management in 1911, he aimed to give managers the information required to minutely control the labour process and combat workers' time-wasting and resistance.[24] But, at Deliveroo, we didn't even have this knowledge in the first place: we started from a position of ignorance, whilst the app collected data in huge quantities. Workers still develop certain kinds of knowledge and skill, despite the despotism of the black box – bike handling, how to get around a city, what shortcuts to take, and the rest – but you never got close to controlling the labour process. The app made all the decisions, because the app had all the information.

The ruling-class understanding of optimal information sharing and cooperation between workers and management today has been somewhat updated from Taylor's original ideas. The neoliberal assault on the workers' movement in the 1970s and 1980s was combined with the development of a new school of management theory: Human Resource Management (HRM).[25] HRM has lived quite a contradictory existence. By 1992, researchers had already identified four mutually contradictory definitions of what exactly it meant.[26] One of the more stable common themes of HRM-inspired approaches was a shift from compulsion to commitment: rather than forcing workers to produce value, workers would be convinced to commit to value production as something they cared about. As a result, the train of thought runs, workers will be happier and better at their jobs, which, in turn, will lead to a situation that is better for 'everyone' (read: the ruling class).

Behind all this there is the echo of Elton Mayo, founder of modern human resources. In the 1930s, he argued that capitalism disrupted the traditional patterns of group formation in society, and led to workers forming irrational and damaging groups with each other (such as trade unions). The solution was to create an alternative and 'rational' way of grouping workers into the capitalist company, subservient to their bosses.[27]

This is the root of the idea of 'commitment' in modern management: workers need to be committed to their bosses, or else they might commit to each other. The possibility of workers refusing to voluntarily 'commit' isn't often considered within HRM, leading to an obvious, but unasked, question: is a dictatorial command to commit really any different from dictatorial compulsion? Instead, the underlying assumption is that workers will always voluntarily commit to bosses who listen to them and cooperate with them.

Deliveroo claims that its workers are committed to flexible work that benefits 'everyone'. But, below the level of propaganda, Deliveroo has a serious problem with commitment. The 'black box' nature of the labour process actually undermines the potential for workers to have much buy-in or pride in their work. Commitment relies on links being built between workers and managers leading to everyone seeing the whole company as a happy family – and these links were exactly what the app prevented. When workers have all the capacity to understand their labour removed and their social cooperation becomes the substance of a faceless system of control, intense alienation is the inevitable result. As deskilled workers with no control over the labour process, who are forced to follow instructions again and again, we became demotivated and uncommitted to the platform. Workers began to understand that we were compelled to do dangerous, difficult, and precarious work in order to make someone else rich. What's more, we all shared this antagonistic relationship with the black box. Hundreds of couriers in any one city were on the same payment terms, did the same jobs, and faced the same (algorithmic) manager. The diverse social group of workers were brought together, into a mass collective subject, through the labour process. The individual members of this collective became increasingly committed to the solidarity we had with other workers through the zone centres and WhatsApp groups. Just as Mayo feared, we were committed to each other, not to the app.

But if couriers don't understand their own work, who does? The most important knowledge about how the labour process and system of control actually function is concentrated in more centralized and better-controlled workforces than couriers: software engineers and app watchers. These Deliveroo workers design and supervise the black box app which manages couriers. The discussion of numerical control above showed how the increased automation of shop-floor machinist labour in the post-war US metal industry involved an increasing division of labour. The machinist, the part programmer, and the coder all cooperated in a complex process, but all of them were artificially divided from one another. As a result, workers were deskilled, lost control of their work, and had their jobs intensified. In this sense, the black box at Deliveroo is comparable to numerical control. In place of the machinist, the part programmer, and the coder, we were the rider, the software engineer, and the app watcher.

The black box is a tool bosses can use to divide workers into two camps: office workers and street workers. We were both invisible to one another. I never thought about the human typing the code which organized my work, and I doubt they thought about the human that received the instructions generated by their code. Deliveroo was totally reliant on the cooperation between two groups of workers, but we barely even realized we were cooperating. Whenever we talked about the app, a lot of couriers couldn't see any difference at all between software engineers and the actual bosses themselves. They thought that our interests were totally antagonistic. But software engineers and app watchers are still exploited and part of the same working class as couriers, albeit a better-paid and differently managed layer of that class. As a result, the vertical isolation of street workers from office workers is not unbreakable. Workers in the tech sector, such as R. K. Uphadya, are discussing overcoming the vertical isolation of software engineers by organizing 'technoscientific' points of production.[28] This organization could be structured industrially (organizing all workers in one industry, rather than all workers in one job role), and so recompose different layers of the working class into one united front against the black box and the bosses.[29] Together, couriers and tech workers would have much more leverage than either group on their own. The disconnect of these two workforces is a key point that allows Deliveroo to systematically exploit workers on the ground and systematically control workers in its HQ.

But industrial-scale organization at Deliveroo could go even further than that: workers in the Deliveroo customer service call centres, cleaning the Deliveroo offices, and guarding the Deliveroo sites all have the same interests as us. Even beyond just Deliveroo, workers in the food service industry at large have the same interests as us: the chefs, waiting staff, and agricultural workers on whom the whole industry relies all also deserve better pay and conditions. When you started thinking about the connections, the potential links between workers across the industry multiplied and multiplied. But the black box existed to try and prevent just that. You are an individual worker, in your individual silo, doing your individual job. Keep your head down and swipe right to accept.

Maybe we didn't control the labour process in any meaningful way, but at least we controlled our own equipment. They might have the black box, but that's all they have, right?

The Means of Subsistence

Whilst I was working at Deliveroo, there was one thing I couldn't work out. I provided the bike, the phone, the electricity, and the mobile data that I needed to work. How did that change things? Did it change things? I had had discussions with interested friends a few times, where I repeated the line that I'd heard other people put forward: 'I basically own the means of production, apart from the app.' Deliveroo is often used as an example of how capitalism is developing a tendency to accidentally hand over the means of production to workers themselves. But it didn't feel like I owned the means of production at all.

Basically, what I was saying to my friends was a weak version of the argument Nick Srnicek makes in *Platform capitalism*. He argues that platforms like Deliveroo outsource the majority of their 'fixed capital' to their workers. Deliveroo doesn't provide bikes, mobile phones, data plans, or insurance. Even when they do provide equipment, like a thermal backpack, they charge you for it. This view has influenced prominent trade unionists in the gig economy, such as James Farrar, general secretary of the IWGB Uber and private hire branch. He wrote in the *New Statesman* that:

> In the old days, the bosses supplied the capital while workers brought their labour and both sides fought it out for a share of the spoils. Today, workers supply the capital and the labour, yet still lose the battle for fairness. Companies like Uber and Deliveroo have mastered technology on such a scale that they have become corporate rent seekers.

This idea – that the gig economy has 'changed' capitalism – is the natural outcome of the conclusion that workers own capital. But what is capital? Above all else, capital is a social relation. That means, capital isn't any one *thing*. Instead, capital is *anything* which plays a specific role in the mode of production. But what role? Well, capital is value which increases in value. In the context of the production of commodities, that means that capital is the stuff the boss uses in order to create commodities that, when sold, will lead to additional value. So, capital is the sum of value contained in the things that go through the cycle that Marx described in *Capital* as its 'general formula': Money – Commodities – (more) Money.[30]

To simplify, if you own capital, then you're a boss and you're making money off workers. So, if the bike of a Deliveroo worker is capital, then the logical conclusion is that they are legitimately self-employed mini-bosses profiting off their own labour-power. Now, that doesn't fit with the experience of working for a platform. Indeed, Farrar has been tireless in taking Uber to employment tribunals and then the court of appeal to argue that he deserves to be paid the minimum wage and holiday pay. So, there has to be some other explanation.

Eventually, I came up with my answer. Instead of representing any underlying shift in the deep rhythms of capitalism, platform capitalism is just a change in its surface arrangement. It is important to understand these shifts in composition, but that doesn't entail rewriting the rulebook. The situation facing platform workers is the same as the situation facing the cleaner who has to bring their own spray, the chef who has to bring their own knife, or the carpenter who supplies their own tools. They don't profit off the exploitation of their own labour – they are forced to buy stuff in order to work. In the case of Deliveroo's moped riders, this often meant expensive hire purchase agreements and delivery driver insurance which locked them into monthly payments for a commodity that devalued rapidly and became an impossible burden if they were unable to work or their bike was stolen. Deliveroo workers were in the same boat as cleaners, chefs, and carpenters, apart from that the stuff they had to bring to work was more expensive.

We didn't own capital – instead, we were forced to include tools used in the production process in our 'means of subsistence' – the stuff we buy with our wages to reproduce ourselves and our labour-power. The amount of value paid as wages is influenced by a lot of factors (like the degree of working-class power, the degree of education embodied in the labour-power being sold, the social norms of consumption, and the rest) but, all else being equal, capitalists won't pay wages higher than the means of subsistence. So, on a wider scale, Deliveroo is part of a trend towards the regressive redefinition of the means of subsistence.

What does that mean? Platform capitalism takes advantage of the weakness of the working class and the fact that a large population just needs whatever kind of work they can get. In the context of a collapsing social welfare system and widespread low wages, there are lots of workers who can't turn down extra work. The bosses and investors of companies like Deliveroo and Uber have *used* this crisis to push back the balance of what the company provides and what the worker provides. For the worker, this push-back is experienced as a reduction in the value of 'elastic' commodities you can purchase – that is to say, the money you spend on other needs beyond bare survival. In platform capitalism, an increasing value of 'inelastic' commodities becomes necessary for you to access work – like a mobile phone,[31] mopeds, or even a Toyota Prius. For Deliveroo workers, this means that our wages were actually even less than they seemed. Once you'd eaten, fixed your bike up, recharged your phone, and paid for your data plan and insurance, you had already paid a lot in order to work. Deliveroo covered the cost of petrol for moped riders in some cities, but everything else was up to us. So, if you did two drops an hour, you might see £8 an hour on your 'invoice' / pay slip, but you'd actually earned £6 an hour after costs – without including the cost of buying a bicycle or moped in the first place. The regressive redefinition of the means of subsistence meant we were all getting screwed even more than was immediately obvious.

This specific phenomenon is just one example of a general problem: for many of us, our wages are covering less and less beyond bare reproduction every month. Workers deserve things like gig tickets, nights out, weekends away, and the rest – but for many, the reality is that it's all a pipe dream. The best you can afford when you are underemployed on minimum wage is sitting on a sofa drinking cans. We're in the worst decade for real wages since the 1790s and the invention of the steam engine. Across the economy, workers are earning less in real terms than they did before the crisis of 2008. Deliveroo workers are just experiencing the particularly sharp edge of a much bigger wedge.

Deliveroo legitimates its claim that its workers are self-employed partly through this fiction that their workers are equal business partners with them. So, the argument that Deliveroo is actually just exploiting workers rather than partnering with tens of thousands of small businesses takes us right to the heart of one of the key questions of platform capitalism: self-employment.

'Independent Contractor' Status

The most widely understood element of Deliveroo's system of control is self-employment. It's relatively common knowledge that one of the characteristic features of platform capitalism is the misclassification of its workers as 'independent contractors'. The claim that workers are self-employed, whilst it might be viable in court, is obviously rubbish to the workers themselves. A survey of Deliveroo workers by the IWGB found that 87.1 per cent of responding workers did not think that the status of 'independent contractor' accurately reflected the reality of the job and 92 per cent felt that being classified as 'self-employed' meant they were 'being treated unfairly compared to an employee' and that 'employers deliberately misuse the "self-employed" category to take advantage of their workers'.[32] On the job, I would sometimes find someone who liked being categorized as self-employed, usually because they believed that if we were given the formal rights associated with employment Deliveroo would immediately go bankrupt. But bogus self-employment is more than just a way to get out of respecting workers' rights, it is an integral part of the system of control.

For starters, it is this status that allows Deliveroo to pay a pure piece wage without any guaranteed earnings. In some cities, like Edinburgh and London, they have sometimes paid seasonal incentives over the months when orders were limited in order to try and retain their workforce, and when they did so it was at a minimum guaranteed rate of 2.1 orders per hour. In those cities, each order is worth £3.75, so the guaranteed rate was £7.87, just scraping over the minimum wage at the time of £7.83. But there was no external compulsion to pay this guarantee – after all, minimum wage is just for employees. On top of that, Deliveroo makes no employer national insurance contributions for their 'independent contractors' to the state, which would otherwise be 13.8 per cent of their wage bill. Money that should be used to support statutory sick pay and pensions is instead used to expand the profit-making apparatus. In Spain, the labour inspectorate got sick of Deliveroo avoiding payments and forced the company to cough up €1.3 million in social security payments, after ruling that Deliveroo workers were employees and not independent contractors.[33] But, in the UK, independent contractor status still stands, despite ongoing legal challenges.

Without employment status, workers lose out on a range of legally enforceable rights. We had no rights to statutory sick pay, holiday pay, or pensions, no right to maternity or paternity pay, no right to vote to force Deliveroo to accept trade union representation, no right to be protected from unfair dismissal, and so on. Almost the entire handbook of employment law goes out the window when employment does. Deliveroo has a long and exhaustive alternative vocabulary in order to reinforce their claim that they, in fact, do not employ their couriers.[34] Intentionally or not, this use of language makes it very difficult for workers to understand just exactly what rights they do or do not have. When I was working, lots of riders were totally unaware that they would have to register as self-employed for tax purposes, and pay tax on any earnings above the £11,000 threshold. Overall, 'independent contractor' status means that workers are dispossessed of both their rights and a full understanding of their legal situation.

The main result of this deliberate assault on the status of workers as workers is a constant feeling of vulnerability. It's not like full legal employment is a state of nirvana – workers are still exploited by bosses, whichever legal category they fall into, and that won't change unless the entire class structure of society changes. But full legal employment status did, for some, seem like it offered protection.

In conventional employment, the state actively regulates the economic relationship between employee and employer. Employment tribunals, legal rights, limits on working time, health and safety laws, and the rest all operate as ways of making sure both sides are playing the (rigged) game. But because workers at Deliveroo weren't 'employees', the state withdrew. Workers quickly came to realize that there was no third party to rely on. Whereas in another job we might have appealed to some external authority when we realized something was unfair, at Deliveroo we had no one to turn to. The situation was as simple as boss vs worker. If we were going to make things any better, we'd have to do it ourselves.

The Menace of the Workers

The organization of work at Deliveroo produced a technical class composition – an organization of individual workers into a working class doing a job – which was ready to explode. We were subject to authoritarian algorithmic management; we had no guaranteed wages; we worked in constant danger; we had no commitment to or control over the labour process; we had no human managers to keep us sweet; we were forced to spend money in order to keep working; and we got no protection from the state. The system of control Deliveroo used to make us produce value was leading to resistance. This resistance was becoming increasingly organized, and an embryonic informal community of Deliveroo workers was now meeting and talking online and offline across the city. The principle that guided these informal groups was a kind of instinctive solidarity, that had yet to tip over into out-and-out collective resistance. We all knew we were against the bosses, but we weren't yet confident in ourselves, the workers. That transition would rely on a process of mobilization and a leap into full-blown class struggle.

4

A Short History of Precarious Militants

In order to understand the mobilization that followed, it's important to understand some history. The use of precarity to control workers isn't a new tactic invented by the ruling class following the latest crisis of capitalism. The phrase 'precarious employment' was first used in the Houses of Parliament in 1812 and was a regular part of parliamentary debate from then until the 1930s.[1] In the history of work in the UK, there are two particularly useful examples to analyse: dockers and builders. The history of these trades allows us to see the concept of precarity from the bottom up – and discover that the idea that precarious workers are weak and disorganized could not be further from the truth. If Deliveroo had kept the militant history of dockers and builders in mind, they might have been more prepared for what was going to happen next.

Dockers

Dock work is one of the archetypal forms of precarious work. Dockers used to wait 'on the stones', standing around outside wharves, looking for work on a purely casual ship-by-ship basis. A constant oversupply of labour was maintained just in case the number of workers needed suddenly increased. When dockers did get temporary jobs, they could be paid by the hour or by the tonne. Working half-days was standard.

As well as being very precarious, these groups of workers were often very tight-knit. The cooperative process of loading and unloading cargo developed an instinctive solidarity between dockers. Stan Weir, US labour militant, docker, and writer, described how gangs of workers formed close bonds as a result of mutually relying on one another during dangerous work.[2] They consolidated these bonds whilst waiting for work, sitting in dockers' pubs, and on the street. When they did get a job, much of their work was done below the hatch of a ship, and so away from the prying eyes of foremen. Gangs of dockers who liked working together would stick together across multiple jobs and get hired as a group. This allowed them freedom to organize and act as they saw fit. Their 'informal work groups' were very strong. As a result, dockers across the world fought for and won a remarkable degree of control of their work, and prevented work intensification making their lives additionally dangerous and stressful. In these conditions, it's hardly surprising that mass militancy was the rule rather than the exception. On a global scale, dockers often led the working-class movement.

A Short History of Precarious Militants

In the UK, the London dock strike of 1889 was famous for winning the 'dockers tanner', a uniform sixpence-an-hour pay rate. Those 100,000 striking dockers were following the example of the match girls of Bryant and May, whose strike against poor conditions in 1888 started the 'new unionism'. The new unionism was a period of rapid development in the British labour movement, which saw the recruitment of unskilled and semiskilled workers, the development of socialist politics within the trade unions, and the use of collective direct action to force bosses to give in to workers' demands. The dockers helped the match girls chart this new course.

By the 1920s, the Transport and General Workers' Union (TGWU) was the official Trade Union Congress (TUC) dockers' union, and the descendant of the union that had been formed during the 1889 strike. But, nonetheless, in 1923, the TGWU bureaucracy signed a sell-out deal with port employers to reduce wages. As a result, 40,000 dockers went on strike. A group of those workers split from the TGWU to form a new union and were ejected from the TUC. By 1927, this union had taken on a permanent form: the National Amalgamated Stevedores and Dockers (NASD).

Following World War Two, dockers finally started to be brought into full-time, regulated employment. The post-war Labour government established the 1947 National Dock Labour Scheme which set up Labour Boards as 'holding employers' for dock workers. They acted as permanent employers for all dockers and would pay any worker without temporary employment with a company a small minimum wage to tide them over. They were 'employers without any work for their employees'.[3] This de-casualization was only partial, and it would only be pushed further when precarious dock workers began to take action again.

Over the years since 1927, the NASD had built a reputation as one of the most militant and democratic unions in the country, and its rank-and-file members consistently took part in unofficial strike action. But it remained small, until history repeated itself. In the 1950s, members left the TGWU in their thousands and joined the NASD following TGWU sell-outs on the question of overtime. In the winter of 1954 alone, 40 per cent of the dockers in Liverpool switched unions.[4] The TGWU bureaucracy threatened to withhold NASD workers' union cards when they were due for renewal in April 1955 to try to prevent them finding work on the docks, until combined strike action by the rank and file of both unions forced them to change their mind. Again, the NASD was expelled from the TUC as a result. This meant that port employers derecognized their union and stopped collectively bargaining with workers. In May, 18,000 dockers launched a strike for union recognition for the NASD. After four weeks of strike action, the TUC were forced to accept the NASD back into the fold. The union was now re-recognized on the London docks, but they held out for two more weeks in an attempt to win recognition on northern docks. Eventually, by a very narrow margin, London dockers voted to go back to work before that recognition was won. Northern dockers responded immediately. They announced their intention to march all the way to London to convince their fellow workers to change their minds. As soon as the London dockers heard of this plan, they re-joined the strike. The strike finally ended in early July. It had been a tooth-and-nail dispute, conducted against both the trade union movement bureaucracy and the bosses. The dockers had only won some of their demands, but an example had been set.[5] Disputes of this kind would continue to flare up again and again on the docks in the post-war period. It was precisely this kind of worker resistance that provoked the 1967 Devlin Report. The bosses and Harold Wilson's Labour government had had enough. There was an industrial relations 'problem' on the docks that needed to be solved.

The solution proposed by the Devlin Report was threefold. First, dock workers would be made proper, full-time employees on a constant wage rate with constant contracts. Second, if they agreed to stop preventing work intensification, dockers would get a big pay rise as part of what was known as a 'productivity deal'. Third, the industry would be consolidated and a massive process of technical recomposition begun in order to reduce workers' power. Basically, it amounted to a massive pay off to workers in the short term in order to change the industry and solve the labour 'problem' in the long term. Both the TGWU and NASD officials accepted the report's recommendations. Rank-and-file workers held out, with unofficial workers' committees around the country, like the Port of London Liaison Committee, rejecting the productivity deal and demanding wage increases without work intensification, but in the end the recommendations were implemented. The state had supported the move because a growing trend towards increased international trade had, in turn, increased the need for efficient shipping and reliably functioning docks. A global logistics revolution was increasing the importance of dock workers by the day. They were situated at a crucial economic node in the network of capitalism, and they had to be bought off in order to stop them using their leverage. Rather than precarious work being seen as disempowering, the bosses and the state understood very well that sometimes precarity means strength. Insecure dock work had shown itself to be a breeding ground for conflict and rank-and-file militancy.[6]

In the long term, the transformation of the industry to reduce dockers' leverage hinged on the massive expansion of 'containerization' in the late 1960s and early 1970s. Rather than cargo being bundled up by dockers themselves, it would be loaded into shipping containers. From this point on, the main job of dockers would be moving those containers on and off ships. The labour process would be changed from top to bottom.[7] The number of opportunities for cargo to go missing – a practice which had for centuries supplemented the income of some dock workers – was also significantly reduced as a result. During this period of huge transformation, worker resistance would not only have threatened to undermine profits or increase the cost of labour. The joint control of workers over the docks could have challenged the reshaping of this vital chokepoint in the economy, and forced concessions in the organization of the labour process which – once fixed into the concrete infrastructure of ports – would be costly and difficult to undo. Containerization had to take place after the neutralization of precarious militancy, or else workers might keep the leverage that the state and employers had just paid so much to liquidate.

Precarious dockers, had, through a near-century of collective fights, shown the ruling class that sometimes precarity is strength. But, as it turned out, not even the change in employment status could pacify the dockers – even after they became permanently employed, dockers retained a residual culture of self-organization and direct action and would continue to do so until the docks were totally technically reorganized.[8]

Builders

At almost exactly the same time as the Devlin Report on dock labour was being written, the exact opposite process was occurring in the construction industry via an invention called 'the lump' – a process which mirrors Deliveroo's tactics of bogus self-employment today.

The lump began in the construction industry in the mid-1960s when the same Labour government decided to try and influence the trade unions in the building industry and restrain them from fighting for significant wage increases. They decided to do so by giving employers tax breaks if they promoted the self-employment of construction workers. These self-employed workers would receive one large lump payment from which they would have to pay tax themselves – hence the term 'the lump.'

These reforms, in the name of the 'national interest', would lead to a huge increase of precarious work in the sector. For builders, you could make more money working on the lump, without the baggage of direct employment. In a boom period, when labour was in high demand, it seemed like a great deal. Often workers negotiating on their own behalf could get a better rate than the unions could collectively. Bricklayers were

79

getting £30 a week via the unions but could make up to £120 on the lump.[9] But, whilst it provided short-term benefits, in the long run it seemed like the lump undermined workers' organization and power.

Due to the nature of the construction industry, constantly moving from place to place with a changing workforce, trade unions had to reorganize every new site from scratch. Every building project started with one big site-wide negotiation led by the trade unions, which determined the wages and conditions on that project. Often sites were run as a 'closed shop'. This meant that the workers would only allow other unionized workers on the site.

But workers on the lump didn't take part in collective bargaining led by the trade unions, and instead made individual deals with the employer. The lump decisively broke the closed-shop model and introduced two parallel processes: the individual negotiations of 'self-employed' workers on the lump, and the collective bargaining of directly employed workers via the trade unions. On some sites, employers even began to refuse to hire any direct employees at all. The workforce in the industry was decisively split. Cumulatively, the breakdown of bargaining also led to the erosion of health and safety standards on building sites. Yearly death tolls in construction regularly went over 200, so that was no small issue. It seemed cut and dried: the lump made workers precarious and undermined the trade unions. From the point of view of workers, it had to be a bad thing.

However, not everyone agreed. The libertarian socialist Solidarity group wrote a famous pamphlet in 1974 arguing against pretty much everyone else in the workers' movement. They argued that the trade unions had created the conditions for the lump to flourish by adopting a negotiating strategy which put the union, the government, and the 'national interest' ahead of rank-and-file workers. When workers on unofficial strike at the Barbican were left high and dry by the construction trade union UCATT in 1967, they said, workers nationally were disgusted. That was why the lump had succeeded in the first place: because workers didn't feel like supporting a sell-out union. They pointed out that the lump also created opportunities for newly precarious militancy: the state now had no idea what payments were going where, workers were taking their own initiative to get a better deal, and the direction of travel in the industry was being set by the rank and file.

Neither argument was conclusively correct. Workers' militancy didn't immediately crumble following the introduction of the lump. The 1972 national construction strike was the largest ever seen in the industry. Workers picketed their own sites and stopped work. A picket is a demonstration by workers and supporters at the entrance to a striking workplace, which aims to prevent that workplace from functioning as normal. Pickets (the people taking part in the demonstration) try and persuade workers making deliveries to turn around, block scab strike-breakers from entering the workplace, and generally apply pressure on the employer. Throughout the 1972 strike, workers also experimented with 'flying pickets'. That is to say, they sent striking workers on buses around the country to picket out non-unionized sites as well. These flying pickets had great success in talking to workers on the lump on building sites outside of the large cities, and persuading them to stop work and

81

join the strike. But after the promising signs of the 1972 dispute, the potential for mass rank-and-file militancy by 'self-employed' workers also didn't manifest itself to the full extent that the Solidarity group hoped for. All that could be said definitively was that, despite increasing precarity and division amongst the workforce, the potential for workers' power wasn't exhausted. Bogus self-employment wasn't going to defeat the possibility of collective action, but it also didn't guarantee it. The lump, in another form, exists to this day. The construction industry still has a workforce divided between the self-employed and the directly employed.

In the case of both dockers and builders, we can see the ongoing contradictions of precarious work. Precarity doesn't necessarily make workers weaker or stronger. Even though it creates conditions where workers are vulnerable, exploitation is heightened, and the power relations between classes are sharpened – it also creates conditions in which workers are keen to fight and have the means to do so. The class composition of the building trade and the docks led to different kinds of precarious worker self-organization, of differing effectiveness, and with differing tactics.

With Deliveroo, then, we are seeing the introduction of precarity in a form that looks something like the lump. But rather than introducing it to split a unionized workforce, accepting bogus self-employment is in fact a precondition of working in the food-platform sector, just as waiting 'on the stones' was a precondition for working on the docks. As an element in a system of control, self-employment increases the vulnerability of workers. But also, as dockers showed, that vulnerability can coincide with a very militant approach.

A Short History of Precarious Militants

Despite all the developments and recompositions of capitalism, the system can never escape its reliance on labour-power. As Marx put it: 'Capital is dead labour, that, vampire-like, only lives by sucking living labour, and lives the more, the more labour it sucks.' That vampiric nature of the system means that its beneficiaries can never abolish workers, the very cause of all of their problems – because if they abolished workers, they would abolish the source of all their profit. Precarious or not, workers are always the precondition of capitalism and have power as a result. As the union song *Solidarity forever* has it, 'without their brain and muscle, not a single wheel would turn'.

But before paying attention to the way that Deliveroo workers used that power to fight back, it's important to understand a little more clearly who exactly I was working with, and what their lives were like beyond work.

5

Workers and Customers

If working for Deliveroo was so stressful, dangerous, and badly paid, why did anyone do it? It's a fair question. To answer it, you need to understand more about the workforce. For most workers, Deliveroo provided an alternative to conventional employment. For one of a number of reasons, they either couldn't get a standard job, or found an alternative more attractive.

Given how grim other jobs can be, a lot of workers liked Deliveroo by comparison. The stress of riding on the road is about the same as, or less than, the stress of working doing 8+-hour shifts in a pub or supermarket. If you're on a moped, it is a much less physically difficult job than if you're a cyclist. You get to be outside all day, constantly moving about, and never have a manager calling you in to cover a closing shift on a few hours' notice. There was a sense of autonomy and independence to the job that wasn't entirely illusory. On a really good day, you could make an hourly wage that was way above what you could earn in a standard job – you just had to accept that there would be bad days too.

Workers and Customers

The stress of the job wasn't always bad. Sometimes you felt like you were in a bobsleigh, getting up to 30-odd miles an hour down a 15 per cent slope and dodging parked cars with the lights of the city spread out below. Because Brighton is built on such steep hills, you would often turn around after completing a delivery to see a brilliant view behind you. At times, it felt like you were a secret kind of city-dweller. If you ride enough shifts doing 20+ miles in circles round and round, you get a deeper sense of a city. You recognize people walking down the street who you've never met before, you accidentally interrupt drug deals and romantic moments, you see the patterns of the rush hour on arterial roads, and you understand the feel of Sunday mornings on suburban streets.

The first hour of a shift always reminded me of the arcade game *Crazy Taxi*. The game was set in a sunny Californian city. There was a constantly ticking game clock, and when you ran out of seconds it was game over. You got time bonuses and scored points by picking up customers and driving them to destinations at break-neck speed, often crashing into things on the way. You'd take a minister to church, a customer to KFC, a fan to the baseball stadium, going from drop to drop for as long as you could. The intentional gamification that was built into the Deliveroo app aimed to reinforce this impression and blur the boundaries between work and play. The black box might be an authoritarian system which ordered around workers like a miniature dictator, but the user interface was shiny.

At Deliveroo, the skilled element of the work was entirely based around riding. As a cyclist, your ability to make use of funny pedestrian routes via parks and up flights of stairs became crucial. The only advantage we had over mopeds was an increased flexibility to cut corners, negotiate one-way systems, use bus lanes, and the rest. I got used to hopping on and off my bike. Sometimes you could get around complicated junctions faster by becoming a pedestrian, waiting for the lights to turn and walking across, depending on what point in the traffic light cycle you were at. Your ability to descend at high speed, fitness, and bike handling were all factors that determined how much you made. The combination of adrenaline, speed, skill, and insider knowledge of routes across the city was intoxicating at times, but once you started to get cold, tired, and bored, that intoxicating element of the work died away pretty fast. So, if that was the positive case for working for Deliveroo, what was the negative one?

Compared to both national and regional averages, Brighton has a higher than average male unemployment rate (5.9 per cent vs 3.3 per cent for the South-East), and lower than average male full-time wages (£550 gross a week vs £621 for the South-East).[1] A similar, although less pronounced, trend applies for female workers. The average monthly price for a single room in Brighton in the fourth quarter of 2017 was £558, up from £380 in the fourth quarter of 2010.[2] With low wages and high rents, workers in Brighton are often under financial pressure.

That's before you even consider the impact of students. Student numbers at Brighton's two universities have risen from 25,000 in 1996 to 35,000 in 2016. That means that about 15 per cent of Brighton's residents are students. If they were all given a maintenance grant that was enough to pay for rent and other essentials, then this population might only create additional demand for labour in the city. But, in fact, most students spend most of their loan on rent and don't have enough left to actually live on. As a result, they need a part-time job just to make ends meet. So, these students flood the part-time, unskilled labour market. Getting a 15-hour-a-week minimum-wage contract at a coffee shop is the gold standard to which most students aspire. Many don't manage to get a job like that, and so end up substantially unemployed. These workers often end up working at Deliveroo as an alternative, and they make up a lot of the cyclist workforce. As a result, the minimum-wage segment of the labour market in the city is highly competitive. Inadequate language skills or a lack of experience are serious barriers to getting work.

The cost of housing only increases the pressure workers are under. Rent is a huge displacing force, with many low-wage workers being pushed out of the city they grew up in. The only way for some workers to stay in the city was to drop out of renting entirely. I knew one Deliveroo rider who found a way to make ends meet by giving up a standard rental contract in favour of becoming a 'property guardian'. He had to leave his home in 21 working days if the property management company he paid rent to told him to, and gave up most of the rights associated with a tenancy. He guarded/rented a room in an old council building, reached by going down a back alley and through a scrap yard attached to a garage. Inside, the vibe was like a Kreuzberg art squat. There were Dali prints on the blue walls, speakers playing soul-inspired 60s pop, and a pair of massive ferns. He paid £200 a month for a room, meaning that he could afford to earn well-below-average wages whilst working for Deliveroo.

He talked about the way that the property management company he rented from and Deliveroo had a number of clear similarities in their models: they both exploited legal loopholes to reduce costs, pretended that their company was a social good for everyone involved, and were run by obnoxious hipsters. It seemed like he had a decent enough thing going – he was paying less than half the rent he would have done otherwise. Renters' rights weren't respected by landlords in the city anyway, he reasoned, so, even if he had a proper contract, he'd still probably get scammed out of his deposit or something. Why bother? It's not like being a full-time employee with a rental contract was so great.

But the cost of rent also hints at why there were so many part-time Deliveroo workers fitting it in as a second job. The wages from one job in Brighton could often prove inadequate, especially for those with caring responsibilities or debts. Most workers ended up at Deliveroo through a combination of positive preference and negative coercion. If you'd given me the choice of working at Deliveroo for an 8-hour shift or at a super-market, I would always pick Deliveroo, but if my main job had paid a bit better, I might not have chosen either.

Migration

The first collective action ever taken by Deliveroo workers was refusing to accept orders from Byron Burgers in protest at how their bosses colluded with the border agency to get workers deported. That's not a coincidence. Migrants were a large, well-organized and militant section of the workforce. Every action taken by Deliveroo workers has pretty much lived or died on whether migrant workers have supported it or not, and the majority of strikes have been catalysed and led by them.

As with Uber, where 19 per cent of the drivers work full-time hours and complete the majority of trips, Deliveroo in Brighton had a core group of workers who were more or less full time.[3] They were often on mopeds, and almost all from South America, Eastern Europe, or South-East Asia. They tended to work consistent hours and would be on the road a minimum of 8 hours a day, 6 days a week. They faced more regular financial pressures than cyclists, often in the forms of families to support and hire-purchase agreements for their mopeds to pay off. That regular pressure meant they worked more and took any fall in wages harder. As a result, they had more workplace leverage and were more committed to consistently decent pay. They therefore were a vital part of the workforce to get on-board if we were going to get organized.

For migrants without the right to work in the UK, Deliveroo could be a vital lifeline. By renting or borrowing an account from another worker, they could work without having to provide a passport. This allowed them to survive within the UK's 'hostile environment'.[4] Likewise, for asylum-seekers without the right to work (who are expected to get by on £37.75 per person per week), working for Deliveroo provided vital extra income. These categories of workers had no opportunity to leave Deliveroo: they could not do another job because they don't have the necessary status. As a result, they were locked into working for the company, experienced no 'flexibility', and were forced to accept sub-minimum wages in order to keep their heads above water. Their desperation rebounded to Deliveroo's benefit.

Closely tied in with migration status, although by no means reducible to it, were language skills. It's entirely possible to work for Deliveroo and speak no English whatsoever. The app works in whatever the phone's operating language is set to, and the labour process requires no extensive verbal communication. Workers who struggled to get other jobs due to their language skills could find work as Deliveroo couriers easily.

With all of this discussion, however, there's some unavoidable confusion. Working in Brighton, I knew there were a lot of Brazilians, Italians, Bulgarians, and Polish working for Deliveroo – but I never actually had a clear knowledge of the numbers. Because the workforce was so big, and turnover was so fast, analysing exactly who worked for Deliveroo, from the perspective of the worker, was near impossible. We couldn't survey a bounded workplace and say: there are X workers from X countries. And, even if we were to understand exactly what proportion of the workforce migrants made up, there is a huge amount of variation within the category of 'migrant'. EU migrants, non-EU migrants, migrants without the right to work, international students – their different statuses all create very different experiences.

One of the clearest ways this became evident was in the knowledge different workers brought to the table. Migrant workers often contributed ideas they had first had contact with through trade unions and strike action in other national contexts. This kind of organic circulation of struggle and knowledge developed a stronger movement. Brazilian workers, for example, often had a very strong understanding of strike tactics. They would be the first to organize pickets and actions as soon as a strike was called.

In this context, with migrants playing a key role in collective worker resistance, it would be easy to bypass the mainstream myths surrounding migrant workers. But doing so would mean not taking the chance to clarify an important point.

There is an idea within socialist politics called internationalism. The essence of it can be summed up in the slogan: 'workers of the world unite, you have nothing to lose but your chains'. Socialists argue that the working class, regardless of nationality, has a common interest in the transformation of society. But this idea isn't universal. In particular, there is one myth that undermines internationalism and that, again and again, gets more of a hearing than it deserves: that migrants bring down wages. This argument fails to understand the fundamental determining factor that sets wages: the power relations between classes.

Under capitalism, bosses always tend to reduce wages to the minimum possible. They want to pay for the minimum means of subsistence required for the reproduction of workers, and nothing more. However, this tendency is controlled by the amount of power workers have. Wage cuts are only possible if workers don't organize to stop them through collective action. When workers are well organized and have lots of leverage, wages can be forced well above that minimum value that bosses aim towards. The reality is that a lack of working-class power brings down wages. When workers aren't organized together, bosses can pay them less. It doesn't matter what the nationality of the workers involved is – what matters is balance of power.

There is, however, a relationship between the balance of power and migration. Bosses can deliberately try to disorganize their workforce by bringing in migrant workers. By undercutting wages and increasing the social distinctions (linguistic, racial, cultural, and national) amongst workers at the same time, bosses can deliberately manipulate the workforce in order to get away with paying them less.

However, the same trick could be played a number of other ways. Across the UK, the introduction of over a million young apprentices earning £2.73 an hour into the workplace has performed exactly this function. The availability of labour not covered by the full adult minimum wage at substantially below the cost of reproduction has done more than migration to keep wages low. Similarly, high unemployment can create a 'reserve army of labour' that bosses can use to threaten their workforce. If you won't accept these lower wages, their argument goes, there are plenty who will. Ultimately, this reveals an underlying reality: the nationality of a disorganized worker is irrelevant. The boss doesn't care whether you're from Warsaw or Warrington – if they can hire you for cheap and you're not in a union, then you will help them keep costs down.

Lots of workers understand, correctly, that the introduction of migrant labour is sometimes used by bosses to reduce wages. But the response of workers to this dynamic on a political level can go one of two ways. The first option is to blame these migrants for the drop in wages. This is the response which the ruling class tries to fuel, because it leads to workers blaming other workers for the strategy employed by the bosses. The result is workers scrapping amongst themselves about who undercut who – meanwhile, wages continue dropping and profits keep rising. However, there are many examples in the history of the workers' movement – particularly during periods of high unemployment like those which followed World War One, and the Wall Street Crash in 1929 – where a second approach has been tried: combatting the use of surplus labour as a disorganizing force through solidarity. In the UK, the National Unemployed Workers' Movement (NUWM) was founded in 1921. The NUWM organized national hunger marches, fought local government officials for better benefits, physically blocked the eviction of unemployed families in rent arrears, occupied factories where the bosses were using overtime rather than hiring, and politically intervened in strikes to support other workers.[5] Solidarity prevented unemployed workers being used as scab labour against other workers and raised the general level of working-class organization. Organization like this, which brings employed and unemployed workers together against the ruling class, overcomes the division of the working class. In the workplace, a response to migration in this tradition focuses on organization: these new workers need to be brought into the fold as quickly as possible, and then a combined fight against the bosses has to be launched to maintain working class power.

So, if you focus on reinforcing the division between migrant and non-migrant workers, you're doing the bosses' job for them. Instead, what's needed is a response to low wages and disorganization which goes to the root of the problem and proposes solidarity as a solution. Moaning about migrants is certainly easier than getting organized, and it might even make some workers feel better for a short while – but, in the long run, it only makes us weaker.

Migrant workers, when they decide to organize, can generate huge leverage very fast. Since 2013, the London-wide cleaners' movement, led by migrant workers, has become increasingly powerful. It has won victories from St Barts Hospital to the London School of Economics (LSE), the *Daily Mail*, city firms, the University of London, the Royal Opera House, and the Barbican. At its strongest, this struggle has morphed from a demand for specific concessions on wages and conditions into a struggle over the respect given to workers. Following an inquiry with some of the striking cleaners at the LSE, Lydia Hughes and Achille Marotta concluded that: 'this struggle for a voice, dignity, and respect is more revolutionary than any demand for better pay or terms and conditions. A wage rise can be negotiated and conceded, but real dignity and respect would require a complete revolution in how the university – and ultimately society – is structured.'[6] So, we can see that migrant workers not only have the capacity to lead a process of working-class organization that can win higher wages – they can also play a leading role in the fight over the shape of society itself. When migrant and non-migrant workers unite, it's a fight we have a chance of winning.

Gender

The workforce at Deliveroo was overwhelmingly male. The ratio of male to female workers in Brighton must have been something like 15:1, judging on observation alone. For those few women, participation in our informal workplace culture could be difficult. One of the very few female workers in the city once came to the zone centre and was immediately hit on by a couple of teenage male workers. Understandably, she avoided the square from then on.

Within a bounded workplace, women would have three choices: either you fight back, put up with it, or move on. The struggle of women over the centuries who made the hard decision and went for the first of these options has been a colossal force for equality and justice. As well as the formal history of the fight for suffrage, there is a deeper history of working-class women's struggle against oppression within their own class, as well as against patriarchal bosses, politicians, and institutions. You only have to read the accounts written by British sociologists in the 1970s and 1980s about the collective culture of women on the shop floor to see that this struggle has a long history.[7] However, within a decentralized and unbounded workforce where women were in the tiny minority, there was another option on the table: just avoid other workers. That option proved to be the most attractive for many women workers, thereby maintaining a gender dynamic which carried through to our later organization. The zone centres were our main recruiting hubs. If female workers began to avoid them, then we were unlikely to recruit them to a WhatsApp chat, and if they weren't on our WhatsApp chats, then we couldn't communicate with them. These chats themselves were also very male-dominated, and sometimes played host to sexist ideas.[8]

So, it's not a surprise that our union meetings were almost exclusively male. The dynamics of gender within the workforce at Deliveroo are a textbook example of the mechanics of class composition theory. The collective failure of male workers to always deal with female workers with respect (social composition) combined with a decentralized labour process (technical composition) to produce a form of worker self-organization which failed to represent the workforce in its entirety and was weaker for it (political composition). It's hard to know much more about the experience of women workers specifically, as a result. Were there women-only WhatsApp groups? Did women workers develop specific organizing methods to combat sexual harassment? I didn't know, and still don't know. In other cities, women played a much greater role in their union branches. The London IWGB couriers' branch was led by women, and women also played an important part in the later development of organization in Glasgow and Southampton. The dynamics that applied in Brighton were not universal – but they were the only dynamics I experienced.

Deliveroo workers in Brighton ended up in the job out of a combination of positive choice and negative economic pressure. They often knew that, if they left, they might struggle to find any similar work in that over-pressured section of the labour market and could end up unable to pay their high rents. Migration status and gender also striated the workforce and produced dynamics that complicated the process of organization.

Overall, the social composition of the workforce could be simplified as follows: cyclists tended to be young UK citizens working part-time to fill gaps in their income caused by the inadequacy of student loans, low pay in other jobs, or general precarity. They made up a big

majority of the workforce, but a much smaller percentage of the total hours worked. They tended to leave the
job after a couple of months. Moped riders, on the other
hand, were usually older migrant workers with limited
language skills and ongoing financial commitments for
bikes, insurance, and supporting themselves and their
families. They were the hardcore of the workforce,
who did the bulk of the orders. These two parts of the
workforce would have to cooperate if any collective
resistance was to emerge.

The Customers

When I started working for Deliveroo, I had an image in
my head of who the customer would be. I had ordered
Deliveroo a couple of times and had just gone for a
cheap pizza, but I knew that I wasn't a proper Deliveroo
customer. A proper customer was a well-paid, Instagram-
conscious consumer, enjoying restaurant-quality food in
an aesthetically impressive minimalist living room. As
I found out, however, the reality on the doorstep was
quite different.

In fact, I *was* a normal Deliveroo customer. A majority of orders were for the cheapest possible food. By far
the most popular restaurants were KFC, Burger King,
and cheap pizza and pasta places. They were all far
more common than gourmet dining. The majority of
orders were placed by normal white-collar workers, not
really hipsters at all – just people with enough room in
their budgets to allow a night off cooking every now
and again. There is a term in Marxist theory: 'social
reproduction'. It means the work required to reproduce

a rested and fed worker ready for another day at work using the means of subsistence. Over time, I realized that Deliveroo made possible the easy outsourcing of social reproduction by sections of the working class with capacity in their budgets. Single parents, people on brutal hangovers or comedowns, workers forced to stay at work late ordering to the office – that's the actual reality of who uses the platform. Deliveroo offers a strange kind of care service: it's Kentucky Fried Chicken tender loving care, KFC TLC.

The platform doesn't just deliver food when you're too tired, short of time, or depressed to cook. It does it in a very particular way. Think about Deliveroo's marketing – if you've ever seen a Deliveroo advert, it has probably been for sushi, Thai food, or a fancy burger. Deliveroo projects this totally unrealistic image of what people use the platform for. In this fairy tale, people order Deliveroo because they fancy a highly expensive restaurant meal, but without any of the atmosphere or excitement that comes with eating in a restaurant. Customers buy into this fairy tale because it's more pleasant than facing up to the reality: you're probably ordering because you're knackered. What Deliveroo is selling is the opportunity to take your inability to look after yourself due to exhaustion, stress, childcare, lack of facilities, skills, and time, etc., and reinterpret it as a luxury. The siren call of Deliveroo is: 'You're not exhausted and struggling, ordering cheap food to your door is actually part of your hipster lifestyle.' As Mark Fisher put it in his essay, 'Good for Nothing':

> For some time now, one of the most successful tactics of the ruling class has been responsibilisation. Each indi-

98

vidual member of the subordinate class is encouraged into feeling that their poverty, lack of opportunities, or unemployment, is their fault and their fault alone. Individuals will blame themselves rather than social structures, which in any case they have been induced into believing do not really exist (they are just excuses, called upon by the weak).[9]

Deliveroo works because, for most customers, most of the time, it provides a high social capital resolution to crises which have been responsibilized. The line of thought goes as follows: you are exhausted and alienated. That is your fault. You should be living a fun and exciting urban lifestyle and consuming fun and exciting commodities, rather than lying on the sofa in your pyjamas in a numb brained Netflix stupor of stress and exhaustion (or maybe a hangover resulting from a boredom-induced binge). But it's alright – there is now a service that delivers fun and exciting commodities to your door! You're not exhausted, you're enjoying a night in.

So, Deliveroo finds its niche in the market in offering a service which resolves the dissonance between two realities. First is the projected reality, created by advertising, that there is a common consumer experience which the urban white-collar worker is meant to participate in. The second is the material reality of a grinding subjection to work and the difficulty of social reproduction, for which you are made to feel individually responsible. With Deliveroo, you can satisfy the social pressure to live up to the projected reality whilst continuing to endure the material reality.

But Deliveroo isn't only ordered to homes. In office contexts, Deliveroo is often part of a wider trend towards white-collar work intensification. A widening layer of workers are now 'treated' to perks in the style of Silicon valley:[10] ping-pong tables for productivity-boosting brain breaks, a free coffee bar to keep your caffeine up, a drinks fridge for a cheeky stress-management beer, an hour extra lunch-break to go to the gym, free breakfast if you get in the office before 9 a.m., your Uber home paid for if you stay after 9 p.m., free drinks Friday after work to increase coercive bonds with your line managers – even (yay) beds in the office! Oh, and, of course, Deliveroo ordered into the office when you work late in the evening, 5 days a week. And all you have to do in return is work relentless 60-hour weeks making your boss rich. These workplaces rely on perk-driven productivity management and soft coercion to squeeze out extra hours of work at way below full cost. A white-collar worker on the salary equivalent of £20 an hour for 37.5 hrs a week (about £30k annualized) who stays an hour later because of a 'free' Deliveroo dinner which costs about £10 is voluntarily accepting a 50 per cent pay cut for the hour. The prevalence and success of food-delivery platforms tells us something about the conditions of life for white-collar workers in the UK.

Figures for 2017 estimate that at least 79 million ready meals and 22 million fast-food and takeaway meals are eaten weekly by adults in the UK.[11] Deliveroo plays into exactly the same dynamics as the other segments of this market, but glamourized. Its success is evidence that a crisis of social reproduction is extending into layers of white-collar workers who previously might have expected greater protection.

As an individual white-collar worker, you have no one to rely on but yourself. You and your co-workers have all been taught to compete with each other to succeed from a young age, through a hegemonic hyper-individualism, intensive programmes of exams, and the graduate job market. As a result, even your friendships at work are tainted by the vague threat of competition. It's normal to work 15 hours a week over contract. Soft coercion forces you to stay in the office late every night. But the worst part is, you are expected to be so, so happy about it. The resulting alienation is profound. This white-collar stasis provokes the realization that your undergraduate dreams are fading, and you're going to have to do this day in day out for the next fifty years – even though it's almost unbearable after just a couple. Because you've got no trade union representation, there is no hope of any solution in the workplace. The only option is to get another job which will be basically the same or slightly worse. But you can't fight back by forming a trade union, because it just doesn't *fit* the culture. You've never seen white-collar workers fighting together in *Mad Men* or whatever other representation you've seen of office life. Every strategy for survival in this context is individual, or, at best, shared with a very tight group. It's a situation which can easily provoke despair.

This was also the flip side of my inquiry, as an office worker at the same time as a Deliveroo driver. I was sitting behind a desk wearing a white collar for nine hours a day, then changing into a turquoise collar a couple of nights a week. I was seeing two sides of a possible working-class alliance. The social division of labour between office workers and Deliveroo workers is obviously a powerful demarcation of one group from another. And, sure, Deliveroo workers in London who do the lunch shift taking £40-a-pop boutique sushi into big trading firms have no class solidarity with the people they're delivering to. But they have much more in common with worse-off white-collar workers. Purely in terms of the relation to the means of production themselves, there exists an underlying possibility for solidarity between the two in the same way that there exists the possibility for alliance between Deliveroo workers and tech workers. As the Greek socialist theorist Nicos Poulantzas put it back in the 1970s, 'organising such strata, incorporating them in trade unions, engaging them in collective practices and demands and breaking the ideology that they are "middle class" or "professionals" is indeed one of the most important stakes of class struggles today'.[12] This professional segment, balancing dangerously on a cliff edge just above the rest of the working class, is no less important today.

The whole system of Deliveroo functions to share the products of social cooperation – by chefs, porters, waiting staff, bike mechanics, software engineers, and couriers – but this process of cooperation is being used to perpetuate a social crisis of scarcity, organised so as to keep making the ruling class more money. In the midst of a widespread crisis of social reproduction, low-skilled precarious workers are put to work delivering food to exhausted and increasingly proletarianized professionals. Despite the ideological efforts made from above to distinguish between different fractions of the working class, all workers are still connected to each other by the social division of labour under capitalism – and we all share a common interest in overturning a class system that exploits us.

6

The Strikes

After a couple of weeks of working at Deliveroo, I wasn't sure that anything was going to happen. On the face of it, it seemed like everything was in the bosses' favour. But as the Italian Workerist Mario Tronti once put it: 'the equilibrium of power seems solid: the balance of forces is disadvantageous. And yet, where the domination of capital is at its most powerful, the menace of the workers runs deepest.'[1] In other words, it always seems like the bosses are on top, until they're not.

The question I began the inquiry with was: why hadn't the strikes spread? My assumption had been that these workers couldn't get organized because of the decentralized nature of the job. I had discovered I was wrong – there was already a pre-existing skeleton structure of WhatsApp/Facebook groups and zone centre meetings which could be the basis for embryonic solidarity. Collective action would rely on turning those networks from chats that focused on helping each other out and sharing jokes into fighting organizations.

I wouldn't have to wait long to see this process in action. Deliveroo began to further increase the labour supply in Brighton in October 2016. More riders started working every evening, but the number of orders stayed the same. That meant that we worked less, earned less, and spent more time at the zone centre. As we stopped going drop to drop, everyone started to get to know each other. I got used to starting work by joining a crowd of between five and thirty workers waiting at the cyclists' zone centre in Jubilee Square.

Jubilee Square is in the North Laine, an older part of the city with lots of small one-way streets and quirky shops. But, unlike the rest of the area, the buildings around the square are all quite recent glass-and-steel developments that house the central Brighton library, a pizza chain, a Mexican chain, a sushi chain, and a fancy independent curry place. Week-on-week, the tone of the conversations we had sitting there became more and more militant. You could see the cogs whirring in people's heads: this was shit, it was the bosses' fault, and we had to do something about it.

These large meetings taking place in a public square created a bit of a strange atmosphere at times. Disagreements could be very fierce: some students could be patronizing, and the other workers weren't afraid to tell them they were wrong, to their face. Sometimes the dynamic would create impromptu speeches, as a conversation got bigger and bigger as new workers arrived at the square. Before you knew it, you could end up talking to a big crowd. Sometimes workers just messed around: one time, workers built a giant pyramid out of thermal backpacks, piling them on top of one another. They shared the photos to our WhatsApp chat.

The cluster of restaurants in the square meant there was always a through-flow of pedestrians going past the crowd of workers. Passers-by tended to be a bit confused about why there were so many of us waiting around. Sometimes it was just strange looks, but it could also turn into active intervention. One evening, I was trying to pitch the idea of a strike to a group of workers. They kind of agreed with me, but there was no collective enthusiasm. They knew that nothing short of a strike would produce any results – but they weren't sure a strike would either. Maybe there was no point fighting at all. We'd all have to call it a day and go get other work. As I made another attempt to push for the idea, I caught the eye of a woman with a couple of children walking past on the other side of the road. She was listening in. 'Go on strike', she shouted; 'we'll support you!' The mood changed straightaway. If random people on the street were willing to fight with us, then maybe we should do something. The fact that we met on the streets, not hidden away behind closed doors, meant that there was always a public dimension to what we were doing. Later, when we called demonstrations, it was remarkable how many people apart from just the workers took part.

As more and more students were recruited, they would sign on for their first shift, obey the app's instructions, and cycle straight to the heart of the organizing process. We'd say hello, give them the low-down, and then start integrating them into discussions of what we were going to do and how we were going to do it. It was a remarkable dynamic, seeing workers from all sorts of backgrounds merging, discussing, and developing together. We were gaining in confidence every day. Clearly, something was brewing.

The Rebel Roo

In the middle of tumult like that, it's easy to push things forwards. Projects that would take months and months of work in difficult times can get done in hours when there is momentum. If I'd learnt anything as a student activist in the years after the high point of 2010–11 had passed, it was that you shouldn't waste that kind of energy. I tried to think of ways we could turn the momentum being created at the zone centres into something more concrete, but I was drawing a blank.

In October, I was headed to Paris. Following the London strike, the left and the trade union movement internationally were keen to know more about how this first massive instance of wildcat action by platform workers in the UK had come about. As a result, Plan C, a political organization, paid for a few Deliveroo workers to travel to a summit of the Transnational Social Strike Platform. The platform brought together unions, political groups, migrant groups, and social centres to talk about coordinating working-class action across borders. At the logistics discussion during the summit, there would be a particular focus on organizing with Deliveroo workers and in Amazon warehouses. Me and two other Deliveroo workers, both of whom were IWGB members who had been on strike in London, got a coach to France together from Victoria. That meant we had two 9-hour journeys to chat, one on the way out and one on the way back, and I intended to make full use of them. On the way there, I found out in detail what had gone on in London. I grilled Mohaan, a moped rider who'd been a key organizer in the strike, about their WhatsApp groups, their protests, their strike fund, and the rest. He also told me about an accident he'd had which had left him unable to work for weeks, and the impact it had on him. For the first time, I was able to talk for hours and hours with a moped rider and begin to understand the differences in work patterns between them and cyclists.

After the assembly was over, we got the coach back. As it wound through the suburbs to the north of Paris, we saw migrant camps made of blue tarpaulins huddled below posters for the fascist presidential candidate Marine Le Pen of the Front National. These camps were right by the edge of the motorway, almost falling into the road.

Me and Mohaan discussed how a concerted effort to push things forward with Deliveroo workers could move the struggle into a new phase. We began to chat through the idea of a workers' bulletin. It could be simple, only a double-sided piece of A4. We'd call it the *Rebel Roo*. Deliveroo loved calling us 'Roos' in their emails, so there was a nice irony in turning their patronizing nickname back on them. The aim of the bulletin would be to circulate information about the technical and political class composition of Deliveroo. In practice, that meant details about payment structures, problems workers had with the app, the kind of bullshit the bosses were telling us to keep us quiet, where collective action had been taken, what tactics had been used, what the unions were doing, and what was proving to be successful.

We'd have to get the tone right. Most workers had a pretty developed 'fuck you' attitude towards the platform but lacked the experience of how to get organized. The bulletin had to be 'fuck you' *and* have a practical strategy. The idea was to pitch it at the level of the most militant workers in the zone centre, just at the forefront of where workers were willing to go. We would have to experiment to find that line. By discussing the bulletin with workers, rather than just handing it out and running away, we could get feedback and work out what the most politically advanced position that could have mass appeal was.

As we got to talking about distribution, we saw the four layers of barbed-wire fences surrounding the roads leading to the Channel Tunnel entrance in Calais. 'The Jungle' camp established on the sand dunes to the east of the city was due to be cleared the next day. The coach passed a chain hotel with a car park full of police vehicles. Vans, lorries, and water cannons, all in the same blue and red. *Les flics* everywhere. Stood on every bridge over the road was a cop, looking for refugees. Someone in Paris had told us how fascist gangs travelled to Calais to beat up people in the jungle, and the police didn't stop them.

About a week later, a friend of mine designed us a parody logo. It was the Deliveroo Kangaroo, but the V-shaped ears were joined by a V-shaped two finger salute, meaning it looked like the kangaroo (i.e. the worker) was swearing at you. We wanted to link it to the two main unions organizing in Deliveroo, so we approached the IWW and IWGB and asked for their support. They happily gave it. The next step was to set up a network of workers to help produce and distribute it. There was no point in writing this thing and putting it out online in the hope someone picked it up – it had to go directly into the hands of workers across the country, and it had to be written by workers across the country. We set up an email account and started to bring together an informal group of writers and distributors from Brighton, Middlesbrough, Leeds, Bristol, Liverpool, Glasgow, London, and a few other places. We even managed to establish very early international contacts with workers in France, Germany, and Italy, who could give us another perspective and more experiences to learn from.

Our informal group was dominated by young cycle couriers, but the bulletin aimed to get beyond that bubble into the whole workforce. As a result, we had translations of an introduction to the bulletin printed in a few languages on every issue: Bengali, Brazilian Portuguese, French, Polish, and Arabic. It read: 'This newspaper exists to help Deliveroo workers in the UK and internationally communicate and organise. Together we can build solidarity and fight for better wages and conditions.'

From the start, the content was pretty much all short reports, no more than 500 words or so, from different cities. If we had a choice between reporting on a city where there was no organization or reporting on a city where there were strikes happening, we always chose the active one. The idea was to develop confidence, and also to learn from the most developed courier campaigns. We collected comparative information on the labour process and the way the company managed us. We learnt that there were at least five pay structures operating in the UK: £4 per drop, £3.75 per drop, £8 per hour plus £1 per drop, £7 per hour plus £1 per drop, and £6 per hour plus £1 per drop. From France, we learnt that Deliveroo sometimes offered guaranteed weekend payments of €15 an hour on Sundays. In cities with hourly systems, an app called 'staffomatic' was used to schedule workers, and a local human manager played a much more important role in coordinating (but not supervising) shifts and the like.

The payment structure you were on seemed to be determined by two factors: the average wage and level of unemployment in the area, and the order volume in the zone. Wherever order volumes were low, there would be an hourly wage. The level of that hourly wage would vary between £6 and £8 depending on average wages and unemployment in the local area. In Middlesbrough, for example, Deliveroo knew that the high rate of local youth unemployment meant they could get away with running a £6 per hour plus £1 per drop pay structure. They ruthlessly exploited labour markets in order to keep their costs down. The bulletin aimed to show how this exploitation was taking place by contrasting low- and high-wage areas. This kind of collective comparison allowed us to begin to argue for certain national demands around pay, such as guaranteed hourly minimums that would apply whatever pay structure you were on.

As soon as the first issue was done, in November, I printed a bunch. I had no idea how distributing a bulletin would go down. Might it look really, well, *weird*? It wasn't an everyday thing. No one had ever handed me a workplace bulletin before. But the idea had come this far – we had to go through with it. The Deliveroo jackets had these inside pockets that were just the right size for about twenty A4 sheets folded in half, and I stashed all my copies in there. I rolled up to the zone centre and started to hand them round. To my relief, pretty much everyone responded positively. The five or so workers sat on the Roo bench all stopped talking to read, looking at both sides. Eventually, we started chatting again. It made sense, they thought. The bulletin allowed the conversation to focus on the experience of the London strike, what they'd done, and how it worked. As more workers turned up, I handed out more copies. Soon I was almost out of the twenty I'd printed. Workers were taking more than one copy, so they could distribute them when they met other riders. I had to ride back to my flat and print another fifty. I hadn't even turned on my app yet. As soon as I did, I started meeting different workers in restaurant kitchens and handing them copies too. Before long, I was flagging down any workers I passed, pulling them to the side of the road to give them one. Over a few shifts, workers began to say they'd already had a copy of that month's one, or they'd read it online. I began to leave a few wedged behind the Roo bench at the zone centre at the start of each evening, and by the time I went home they'd be gone.

This went on for a couple more months, getting more successful all the time. Friends from Glasgow who'd started working for Deliveroo said that the link for each new issue was being shared in their WhatsApp groups. I began to believe that there really was an opportunity for a second wave of Deliveroo strikes and to start the fight against the company again. The bulletin was contributing to the growing collective political knowledge and consciousness of workers. We were educating ourselves from the bottom up. Our email account was getting emailed every few days by a rider who wanted some copies sent to them to distribute in their zone. By January, our combined online and offline circulation had topped out at about 1,500. That meant that something like 5–10 per cent of the 15,000-strong Deliveroo UK workforce was somehow in contact with the *Rebel Roo*, depending on what assumption you made about how effective our distribution network was at getting copies into workers' hands. The *Rebel Roo* was everywhere, and the rebellion wouldn't be long coming.

The First Meeting

The new year came and went. On New Year's Eve, a friend had said to me that she was afraid of how 2017 would go. The general mood was pretty bleak. It felt like everyone was being stalked by the black dog. For Deliveroo workers, the major problem was that wages had fallen dramatically. It was now not uncommon to do one delivery an hour, even during peak evening periods. A couple of months back, you could make £12 an hour from 5.30 p.m. to 10 p.m. Now the average was more like £6 to £8 an hour. The discussions at the zone centre got more bitter, more purposeful, and angrier. We set about organizing our first meeting. We booked a room in a community centre for the end of January, asked an IWGB representative to come down from London, and started to spread the details online and in person. I got a lot of workers say that they'd be there, but I'd organized campaign meetings before. I knew that 'I'll be there' only really meant 'there's a 30 per cent chance I'll be there'. On the morning of the meeting, I told myself I'd be happy with over five people turning up.

When I opened the door, a couple of minutes early, I was surprised. Some riders were already there, setting the chairs out. There were five of us, and it wasn't even meant to start yet. More and more workers kept walking in the door, until there were twenty couriers and a couple of supporters in the room. We'd mostly met before, at the zone centre or in sweaty restaurant kitchens whilst waiting for food – but this was the first time I'd ever seen any of them outside of work. We were almost all cyclists, with only a couple of moped riders. The atmosphere in the room was strange. Everyone knew this could be the start of something. Together we talked about our problems with the job, and a flood of ideas for demands emerged. Everyone had something specific they wanted changed: from the amount of time you wasted 'on hold' to the call centre when a delivery went wrong, to the state of the kit, to the triple orders which were bad for the customer, to the lack of discounts at local bike shops, to the rates of pay. The demands to solve those problems varied wildly. Some workers wanted a wearable video camera to be a standard part of the kit so that if an accident took place we'd all have a record of it; others wanted insurance deals, an £8 guarantee for the first hour you logged on, a £12 guarantee for all the time you were logged on, more call centre staff, and on and on. The attitudes towards management were all over the place. A few workers thought that Deliveroo would voluntarily recognize a union branch if we set one up; others thought they'd fight us tooth and nail. We worked out that we were paying about £2 an hour in costs just to be at work, which made the wages look even worse.

Slowly, the room agreed to form a union branch and establish some concrete demands. Migrant workers with some prior experience of corrupt unions wanted guarantees that their subs wouldn't be wasted, that the union wasn't secretly connected to the bosses. The IWGB representative was Max Dewhurst, the same rep who'd seen Dan Warne humiliated by a crowd of workers in London six months ago. They told us that we'd have to do a hell of a lot of hard work to get a branch organized – but, pending some changes to the union constitution to allow us to form a branch outside of London, we could join. When the meeting heard about the victories the IWGB had won for outsourced cleaners in London, it became clear that it was the kind of union we wanted to be part of: active, militant, and direct. I told the meeting that the *Rebel Roo* was now in touch with fifteen cities where some kind of organizing effort was ongoing, be it an isolated person distributing the bulletin or a fully established union branch. Deliveroo only operated in about sixty cities in the UK at the time.

Everyone started wrapping their heads around the fact that, because we weren't technically employees, Deliveroo had no legal requirement to recognize our union. But, at the same time, all legal restrictions on strike action no longer applied. Yes, we had no access to sick pay or holiday pay or formal employment rights – but we also had no obligation to give employers notice that we were going on strike, or to conduct a postal ballot. We could use workplace democracy in its most immediate form to decide our course of action. This wasn't as confusing as it could have been, given that very few people in the meeting had ever been members of a trade union before. We didn't know what the formal processes were, so totally ignoring them and going by common sense instead wasn't a problem for us. Suddenly, we began to understand how precarious conditions could be a source of strength. We had almost no experience of organizing a workplace, let alone being on strike – but that didn't matter.

All the laws that had been passed over decades and decades to restrict the rights of workers to organize and take action in the workplace were based on the idea that they were regulating the employment relationship. But the employment relationship was precisely what Deliveroo had undermined. The 2016 Trade Union Act – a piece of legislation so draconian that Oxford law professors called it 'authoritarian'[2] – was out the window. It would be a straight fight: bosses vs workers.

The February Strike

At the meeting, six reps were elected to lead the organizing effort. I was one of them. We had an idea of what to do next. We'd start small, getting a membership database together and setting up a union WhatsApp chat. After recruiting a few more people, we would start some action, building slowly. Our idea was to all stop wearing the uniform. We'd cover over the logos on our box and take their branding hostage. Then, maybe, we could think about calling a demonstration. We were going to take it very slow.

The rest of the workforce had a different idea. Brazilian moped riders who'd heard that a meeting had been held and a union branch formed decided that the pace needed to be forced. Their WhatsApp group chat was the origin point of calls for strike action on the first Saturday evening in February. When the message started getting out there into other chats and being discussed at the zone centre, other riders seemed to agree

115

that action had to be taken soon. There was no time to waste. Before long, details were being communicated back and forth, and the strike was gradually endorsed by more and more of the workforce. A strike committee of union and non-union cyclists and moped riders was established, which would meet a few days beforehand to plan things. The nascent union backed the strike as soon as we heard about it. The whole thing was kept secret: Deliveroo wouldn't know anything until the app came crashing down.

There was only one problem: I was going to be away. I had a family commitment which meant I was going to miss the strike completely. I'd have to keep up with everything via WhatsApp and Twitter on the train home. I was gutted to miss it. It was all anyone was talking about.

The day came, and over 100 workers met at Jubilee Square. I saw photos of the zone centre more packed than ever before. There was no space, just mopeds and bicycles everywhere. IWGB officials, including the general secretary Jason Moyer-Lee, came down from London to support the strike. Along with the reps, they began to hold an exceptional general meeting of the branch to set our demands. After just half an hour, the app was in meltdown. Restaurant workers later told union reps that orders had been delivered 3 hours late, and that order volume had collapsed by over 50 per cent. Food was stacking up in the kitchens, and no one was turning up to deliver it. The emergency general meeting voted unanimously to unionize and make three demands of the company: (1) a pay rise to £5 a drop; (2) a hiring freeze; and (3) no victimization of union members. Deliveroo was given two weeks to respond.

The Strikes

After that vote, the strikers set off across the city in a giant convoy of mopeds and bikes.

After that first strike, everyone's mood changed. Workers started to decorate their backpacks and boxes with huge motifs. They spent loads of effort on converting the Deliveroo logo into a modified poster with an angry, scratched-up Kangaroo-worker and the slogan 'Deliveroo a living wage'. We took back the advertising space for ourselves. Conversations at the zone centre were buzzing with people telling stories about the strike. People like me who'd missed it were hanging on every word.

Deliveroo's immediate response was to send down managers to set up one-on-one meetings at a chain cafe which overlooked the zone centre. Some workers booked sessions to discuss the demands of the strike. I didn't bother because I felt like they wouldn't change anything unless they were forced to negotiate, and, anyway, I was at work during the day. It seemed like the only purpose of the whole thing was to diffuse the anger directed at the platform. Some riders took in a laundry list of complaints and got hardly any concessions. A few union reps attended together in an attempt to convert the discussion into collective bargaining, but the Deliveroo representatives refused.

It wasn't just Brighton workers who were excited by the strike. Workers in Leeds who had been organizing with the IWW took heart from our example. They had begun organizing in similar conditions to us, as their pay declined. They were an hourly paid zone, and many of them were facing cuts to their regular hours week-on-week. In December, rumours of a move to a full piece rate had led to a concerted effort to organize.

They built a union base of around thirty workers. Then things started to go wrong. Two of the main union organizers in the city had their contracts terminated, and five more organizers had their fixed hours cut even further. However, they didn't give up. They launched a campaign of strikes and demonstrations demanding the changes were reversed. As a result, the terminated organizers were given their jobs back, and the rest had their hours returned to normal. The local manager moved on to become the area manager for York.

In this context of increasing national pressure, the IWGB in Brighton organized a number of 'Ride with Us' demonstrations. These demos all stuck to a similar pattern. Workers and supporters rode around some of the most popular restaurants in the city. At each stop, we'd have a speech outside, block the road for a bit, and send a delegation in to try to get the restaurants to sign up to support our demands. This only really worked when we talked to regular workers rather than supervisors, but it was good to have pressure on the supply chain as well as on Deliveroo. If their restaurant partners started giving them grief about their workplaces being disrupted, that gave us more leverage.

One of my good mates came along to support one of these demonstrations on one of the worst bikes I've ever seen. It was a huge steel Dutch-style bike, designed for a country with no hills. It was shared between his housemates, and they took turns using it to get to work without paying for the bus. They were all skint and didn't have the money to get it repaired, so the chain was basically one long piece of rust. It would fall off at regular intervals, whenever he went over a speed bump. It had a big woven shopping basket on the front, into which he had strapped two big flags. He looked like a muppet, but it was good to have him there. We met at the zone centre, then set off on a tour of the city. Someone set off a smoke flare as we were climbing up Trafalgar Street towards the station, and the burning embers landed on my bare arm. I had a flag in my other hand, so I couldn't brush them off, I just had to grunt and wobble my way up the street whilst my skin sizzled.

The demo wound around the south Laines, before turning back and heading towards where we started. I was part of the delegation of workers that went into a posh restaurant. The orders from there nearly always went up a massive hill into Hove, delivering to quite fancy family homes. They had a habit of making you wait in the underground parking garage that connected to their kitchen for anything from 5 to 45 minutes. Those waits meant we lost out on orders, and during a peak period could totally sabotage your earnings for the whole night. All in all, it wasn't my favourite restaurant.

As we went in, we were met by a panicked supervisor. He hurried over to us, looking like he thought we were about to start breaking things. When I tried to explain what we were doing, his mood changed. *We* wanted something from *him*. He looked like he enjoyed saying no. I lost my patience, and more or less told him to shove it. We must have made that restaurant tens of thousands of pounds, if not more, by lugging their food across the city whilst being exploited to the hilt. For months, this loser had seen groups of workers gathered outside the door in the freezing cold because they had no work. And now, when we finally came to them and asked for them to just put their name on a piece of paper – that was too much. We were learning that even 'independent', 'local', and 'authentic' businesses were still businesses. Their supervisors and bosses still valued a close relationship with Deliveroo over the conditions of the people who worked for them. A hipster burger restaurant responded in exactly the same way, and another rider lost his rag at them.

The final big demonstration we held during my time at Deliveroo was 'Precarious Mayday'. It happened in the middle of the snap general election campaign. Theresa May and the Tories thought they were on their way to wiping the floor with Corbyn's Labour. After all, they called the election when they were 20 per cent ahead in the polls. In fact, they were in the process of making a historic mistake. The idea behind the demo was to bring together students and workers to make a bigger political point about how work wasn't just bad for Deliveroo riders, it was bad for everyone. Given the context of the election, it seemed like people would be listening. The three main blocks were Deliveroo riders, precarious academic workers, and supermarket shelf-stackers. It was a pretty broad coalition, with everyone from a soon-to-be Labour MP to anarchists making up the numbers.

A few weeks later, I was in my mate with the terrible bike's living room. We were watching the election results. As soon as the exit poll came out, we were in a state of shock. It looked like the Tories were going to lose their majority. I went to the nearest Co-op and bought a load of extra booze. The newly left-wing Labour party, who were meant to be headed for total disaster, had actually increased their vote share by 10 per cent. But the sweetest moment of all was when Nick Clegg, the liar who made us pay £9,000 a year to go to university, lost his seat.

A Second Strike

But, however well the election had gone, the situation in the workplace was still tough. Over the summer, our campaign collapsed.

Strangely, the collapse happened when we won an unofficial hiring freeze right around the time of our Mayday demonstration. That might sound counter-intuitive, but the slowdown in recruitment led to an increase in orders per hour. That partially resolved the wages issue, which demotivated riders from keeping on fighting. At the same time, we became busier, which meant we spent less time at the zone centre, which took away one key opportunity to talk. A lot of student workers who we'd organized alongside went home or graduated. The union branch became non-functional, and constant rapid turnover meant a load of the original strikers left the job. When the hiring freeze ended a couple of months later, a load of new, non-unionized riders began to work, diluting the organization of the workforce.

In an attempt to solve the labour oversupply problem and the antagonism it caused, Deliveroo began to change the way the 'black box' of the app worked. In early 2017, a 'pulse' system started to be trialled amongst riders. This pulse was meant to indicate demand by showing order volume on a scale from low to very high. Essentially, it took a function of the already-existing WhatsApp chats, and integrated it into the app itself. But this time, rather than other workers answering the question, it would be the bosses. Workers didn't trust it from the start. When we met at the zone centre, we would compare what our pulses were saying. I could have very high, and other workers could have low. We were in the same zone, standing next to each other, but apparently demand was totally different. Comparison proved that we weren't being provided with unfiltered data about demand, but actually there was some element of hidden labour management built into the pulse. But, as time went on, an increasing proportion of riders were accepting it as gospel. It began to dictate their work schedules, and as it was tweaked and improved over time even the sceptical riders began to rely on it.

The culture of cyclists meeting at the zone centre was in sharp decline. The chain sushi restaurant took away the Roo bench we had used to sit on. Evidently, they didn't like us cluttering up their shop front. They still needed us to do deliveries, though.

The zone centre was never totally created by the demands and organization of the labour process. You needed to be in the city centre, sure, but that was much bigger than Jubilee Square. There were some restaurants in Hove which were miles away from the zone centre, and if you wanted to deliver from them it made sense to wait somewhere else. The app instructed you to go to Jubilee Square, but you could always ignore the app. I started to see more workers waiting on their own. Most of the time, this meant they just locked up by the side of the road near the centre of town and went on their phone. The zone centre, in retrospect, had actually been part of our workplace culture. We all met there because we *chose* to meet there.

It was quite possible to work for Deliveroo and steer clear of all your co-workers. Robbie Warin, a researcher who interviewed Deliveroo riders in Brighton whilst I was working, found some workers who took this approach back in January/February of 2017, just as the union was starting.[3] But, in the months since, an increasing section of the workforce seemed to decide to steer clear. There seemed, at a distance, to be a few reasons behind it. Either they'd just started, and the collective workplace culture was so broken down that they didn't even know that it had existed, or else they had grown tired of developing rapport with co-workers only for turnover to get rid of everyone they knew within a month. I'm sure some preferred to work in isolation, just them and their phone, because that's what suited their personality. Any way you looked at it, though, this acceptance of individualization broke down the solidarity essential for an effective strike.

Cyclists' earnings had fluctuated since the first strike; when the hiring freeze ended, they definitively declined. Workers speculated that the algorithm was allocating more deliveries to moped riders and de-prioritizing cyclists. Because of the piece wage system, this meant that mopeds were raking it in whilst cyclists couldn't get orders. There were a few possible incentives for Deliveroo to push this change in the labour process. Despite having to pay a petrol bonus, mopeds were generally quicker, especially in a city as hilly as Brighton. They also worked more consistent hours so could be more reliable. It could even have been an automatic function of an inbuilt machine learning process, which deprioritized slower workers in favour of faster ones – thereby systematically favouring mopeds.

However, it didn't escape our attention that our union branch had been made up primarily of cyclists. Participation in the strikes had been much more even, but the IWGB organizing group in Brighton was almost all cyclists. The perception amongst the veterans was that cyclists had begun a fight against low pay, and, as a result, our part of the workforce was being forced out. That kind of mass victimization of an entire segment of the workforce – whether real or perceived – was a powerful disincentive for organizing. The situation was analogous to a mass redundancy for a well-organized car plant, but with none of the transparency. The workforce was divided into two by this change, and the distinctions in the social composition of the workforce along lines of education and migration status exacerbated the division. Because we had no idea what went on inside the app, there was no definitive way of responding to this theory: we couldn't just assume it was true and begin campaigning on that basis, but we also couldn't absolutely say that nothing had changed. The black box left us in the dark.

A lot of key unionized workers began to drift away. Those who remained bought mopeds. I started a Ph.D. and began teaching seminars shortly after. I didn't have as much time to work anymore, and, anyway, it seemed like the whole organizing drive had gone belly up. There was no point working anymore with the cyclist pay as bad as it was. The moped riders decided to use two new informal zone centres in better locations: one nearer to Burger King and KFC on Western Road, and one outside the McDonald's on London Road. When I walked past Jubilee Square, I rarely saw anyone there. Sometimes I'd bump into a worker I knew and chat, but the time of mass meetings had passed. People stopped using the old WhatsApp groups. It seemed like things were going quiet. Maybe the struggle had been a one-off.

The Strikes

In July, the government-commissioned Taylor Review on Modern Employment Practices reported back.[4] It had been told to look at the development of the gig economy and the way it challenged conventional employment practices. Unsurprisingly, given that a quarter of the review panel were Deliveroo investors, it made a load of recommendations that added up to a sum total of nothing. The IWGB's response to the report was titled 'Dead on arrival'. It was a 64-page demolition.

The union's analysis of the panel conducting the review claimed that: 'your panel members were biased and/or unethically conflicted, your panel had no worker or trade union representation, you refused to meet with the IWGB despite our direct stake and experience in the issue at hand, you incorrectly portrayed the current law, and you often ran the employers' preferred narratives'. The union ridiculed Taylor's writing style, did everything short of accusing him of being a Tory stooge, and rubbished the vast majority of the review's proposals:

> out of the Review's 52 proposals [sic], we choose not to comment on 15 as we lack the relevant expertise or direct experience of the issues they seek to address, 17 are so bland or devoid of substance or teeth we feel we cannot really assess their supposed value, 12 would probably do no harm but also won't achieve a whole lot, 4 are a mixed bag – containing both good and bad elements, 2 are bad, 2 have potential to be good but are so devoid of detail the likely impact is difficult to assess, and 1 recommendation we can wholeheartedly endorse in its current form.

That one endorsed recommendation? That the government should 'build on and improve clarity, certainty and understanding of all working people by extending

the right to a written statement to "dependent contractors" as well as employees'. In practice, it meant
Deliveroo workers should be able to ask for a paper
copy of their contract in the same way as employees
can.[5] It was hardly transformative.

October came around and thirty workers in Bristol
struck over unpaid wages, and won almost immediately.
They weren't connected to the IWW branch there, but
it was nice to see that workers hadn't given up. I didn't
think there was any chance of something like that happening in Brighton, though.

Then, in November, the IWGB lost in court. The
union had taken a case forward demanding the right
to represent riders in the Camden and Kentish Town
zone, as 'limb b workers' (a specific sub-category of
self-employment). The Central Arbitration Committee
decided that they could not do so because, whilst they
met all the other standards necessary to force Deliveroo
to accept trade union representation, the right to 'sub-
stitute' meant that Deliveroo workers were classified
as independent contractors, not self-employed workers.
Because they could theoretically allow someone else to
use their phone to do orders, they weren't legally enti-
tled to have a trade union represent them. Dan Warne's
response was that: 'riders enjoy being their own boss'.
Of course, that was easy to say, when he was their
actual boss. Not only had our organizing drive gone to
pieces, so had the latest stage of the legal campaign.

But then, a few days later, the old WhatsApp groups
had their first messages in months. When I started getting notifications, I had a look to see what was going on.
A strike had been called. Just like last time, it was an initiative that started with the migrant moped workers. Pay

had fallen again, for everyone, and they were fuming. At 6 p.m. on 25 November 2017, a second strike would take place. The remains of the IWGB branch rushed to do what we could to help prepare. We drafted a petition to Deliveroo management that could be signed on the day, and decided to join the picket.

Just after 6 p.m., fifty workers met on the Old Steine. Any Deliveroo riders going past were flagged down and convinced to join the strike. I pulled over a teenager who was working with Deliveroo whilst at college. I knew him from our first organizing drive, and he'd always been supportive. I told him it was a strike, and he wavered. I could see in his head that he was debating carrying on working. He told me he needed the money this month – Deliveroo wasn't paying as well as usual. 'That's why there's a strike', I said. He nodded, locked up his bike, and joined the picket. The crowd grew, bit by bit. The few workers who decided to scab were chased for the 10 metres to the junction. One furious picket had a favourite heckle he used every time a driver ignored us: 'Don't you get how this works?'

Deliveroo opened up an 'Editions' kitchen just before I started my Ph.D. An Editions kitchen, more accurately known as a dark kitchen, was basically a site owned by Deliveroo and hired out to busy restaurants so that they could run a second, delivery-only operation and increase their sales. It was situated in Hove and was very small compared to the size of the dark kitchens in London.[6] As soon as the strike began, the workers sent pickets to stop it working. These pickets did their job well, and within minutes the shutters were pulled down and the kitchen was closed. The chefs had walked off the job, either in solidarity with us or because they realized the pickets would make deliveries from that kitchen impossible. It didn't really matter either way. The workers knew, from their experience of the job, where they needed to put the pressure on.

Just as it had done during the first strike, the app stuttered and then collapsed. 'Not seeing your favourites?' it asked customers; 'We're very busy in your area right now.' Deliveroo was telling the restaurants that riders were 5 minutes away. They kept on promising that a rider was assigned and would arrive eventually, even though the strike meant that there was no one to deliver the orders. As a result, chefs kept on making and remaking the same orders over and over again, only for the food to go to waste. Kitchens across the city were in chaos. Standing just behind the picket line, chatting and joking, was a small group of us who'd been IWGB reps the first time round.

This second strike proved something: even if the union branch falls apart because the activists get other jobs, and it starts to look like we only won some small temporary concessions, that doesn't mean everything is over. Organically, out of the networks of workers and the experience of the job, resistance emerges again. The class composition of Deliveroo means that workers can't put their feet up. Unmediated struggle between workers and bosses has to continue, or else the situation gets worse. Without the stability ensured by a contract, the terms of work are constantly up for renegotiation. The bosses are always hungry for more profit. As one *Financial Times* commentator put it: 'not offering employment benefits such as sick pay and paid leave reduces labour costs by an estimated 20 to 30 per cent, but the industry remains ripe for cost-cutting and rationalisation'. The reality of that cost-cutting, on the front line, is a constant class struggle.[7] Will workers get paid enough to pay rent and eat? The determining factor is the strength of their constantly renewed self-organization. As a worker on the picket line in November put it: 'We have to fight or else they fuck us – there is no other option.'

These fights didn't just kick off in the UK. The strikes which began in London in 2016 spread across Europe and farther afield. The first city to react was Turin, where workers responded to the London strikes by calling their own, in a fight over wages. Then it went quiet. From the vantage point of the winter of 2016, the action looked like a blip. But as I realized whilst I was on the job, these strikes had deep roots. The second wave of UK mobilizations in Leeds and Brighton began in February. At almost the same time, French workers mobilized on a large scale in Marseilles and Paris. This time the action spread even farther. Workers in Germany had their first mobilization in Berlin; Spain saw a first national coordinated strike across three cities: Barcelona, Valencia, Madrid, and things kicked off in France again: Paris, Bordeaux, Lyon. Then came the third wave. Mobilizations took place in Brighton, Amsterdam, Brussels, Bologna, Turin, and Berlin all in the same month, November 2017. The struggle continued into the new year. Mobilizations also took place in Hong Kong and Australia, and French workers went on strike during the 2018 World Cup final. Their slogan? 'We will fight like Mbappé', France's top-scoring 19-year-old winger.

In China, the first half of 2017 saw militant action being taken by food-platform couriers. Meituan, one of the world's ten largest start-ups, is a food-delivery platform similar to Deliveroo but at much larger scale. Whereas Deliveroo is valued at $2 billion, Meituan is valued at $53 billion.[8] Its workers make a colossal 13 million deliveries a day. They were also responsible for 11 per cent of total strike action in the service sector in China over the first half of 2017.[9] The average Meituan courier is a middle-aged ex-factory-worker, ejected from the shrinking industrial sector of the Pearl River Delta and forced into the expanding urban surplus population which relies upon hyper-precarious gig work to survive.[10] They rush across cities like Shenzen at dangerous speed to deliver food to the new white-collar tech workforce employed at companies like Tencent. These platform workers, often veterans of fights in their factory jobs, end up grappling with the familiar problems of work intensification, safety issues, and low wages in a new context. The resulting strikes are often nationally coordinated across platforms, and sometimes result in violent confrontations with the police.[11] Across the world, the expansion of food-platform work has led to the expansion of food-platform worker resistance. The fundamental dynamics we experienced in Brighton were the same as those experienced by workers in the Pearl River Delta.

Invisible Organization

Romano Alquati – an Italian workerist and sociologist – developed the concept of 'invisible organization' to suggest that the 'spontaneous' emergence of strikes at FIAT manufacturing plants near Turin in the 1960s were actually not very spontaneous at all. Instead, he proposed that the strikes were the result of a non-union form of self-organization which was invisible to external observers, including the union itself.[12] The same concept applies almost exactly at Deliveroo. Our invisible organization had two channels: the WhatsApp groups, and the zone centres. I've already described how both of these worked in practice, but now it's possible to reflect on their operation in the abstract.

The possibility for worker self-organization via invisible channels enabled by mobile technology hasn't been lost on union-busting bosses. Alfred DeMaria 'specialises in combating union organisational campaigns and in developing programs to keep companies operating in a union-free environment'.[13] He is, in short, a leading scab lawyer. DeMaria has written in a union-busting journal that: 'Employer awareness of how employees can use new media tools, including social media and dedicated apps, to interact among themselves and with union organizers is absolutely necessary for maintaining nonunion status. Employers who ignore this *potential stealth activity* risk their union free status' [emphasis mine].[14] Alquati's concept of invisible organization has a parallel in the bosses' own literature.

The 2018 Brazilian truck strike was one of the strongest examples of this phenomenon so far. The deregulation of diesel prices by the neoliberal government of Michel Temer, which came to power after leading a congressional coup against the leftist Dilma Rousseff, led to a 38.4 per cent increase in prices and the subsequent explosion of a huge national strike. The drivers who operate Brazil's fleet of 1.6 million trucks set up 600 strategic blockades on major highways. Shutting down logistics strikes at the heart of modern capitalist societies. Trucks move 60 per cent of the goods transported around Brazil, and, as soon as they stopped running, shortages ensued. Supermarkets ran out of eggs, potatoes, and tomatoes, and petrol stations ran out of fuel. Airports were closed, and bus services cancelled. The whole strike was coordinated via WhatsApp groups, with official unions entirely side-lined.[15] The highly porous nature of these channels creates the possibility for organization to increase in scale at incredible speeds, but also confuses processes of political representation: parts of the movement were calling for a military coup, whilst others were socialists. That diversity of views is perhaps an inevitable part of a strike movement with such a fluid organizational form. Importantly, many Brazilian migrant workers who took part in invisibly organized food-platform strikes in the UK saw a parallel organizational form being used to huge effect back home. Evidently, the examples of invisible organization at Deliveroo have not even approached the most incendiary potentials of the form. Fragile logistical systems plus rapidly scaling invisible organization results in a flammable mixture.

The other channel of invisible organization was altogether more old-fashioned. A repeating dynamic of piece work in a workplace with elastic demand for labour was that it required a pool of unemployed labour on standby. That labour needs to be concentrated in a specific place, so that it can be easily called upon. However, the workers waiting there earn nothing and are unsupervised. As a result, these labour reserves become central points of organization. Minneapolis logistics workers in the 1930s, who organized with the Teamsters union, waited in 'the doghouse'. In the London docks, it was 'on the stones'. For Deliveroo riders, it was the zone centres.

In July 2018, a strike broke out in Southampton. Thirty Romanian UberEats riders drove to the Southampton office to hold a demonstration during a strike over low wages. Without a boost they were being paid as little as £2.80 a delivery with no hourly rate. They'd been promised four drops an hour when they joined; the reality was nothing like it. They wanted a guaranteed hourly rate, a decent boost, and bonuses for working in extreme weather. They wanted their demands to be met within a week, or they'd strike again the next Saturday.

It was an impressive-sized strike in a smaller city. There was just one thing. The cyclists had been organizing too. Without any idea that the mopeds were angry or talking about taking action, the cyclists had spent the last month trying to form a union branch. The invisible organization could be *so* invisible that two parts of the same workforce could be oblivious to parallel organizing efforts. The social and technical divisions within the workforce hadn't prevented the emergence of collective action, but they had limited it. As soon as the fight was in the open, the different groups linked up and began to cooperate. It wasn't just the bosses who could be confused.

Politics

Mobilizing for strikes and protests led to us developing some basic common political ground as a workforce. We agreed that workers had more in common with each other than with bosses, and that we would only improve our situation by putting pressure on them. But this common sense didn't really translate into formal politics.

The key organizers within the cyclist workforce often had some kind of experience in the social movements that emerged after 2010. This was where I fitted in. The student and anti-austerity movements had given us a common set of ideas and tactics. In the realm of 'big P' politics, we were all socialists of one kind or another. Within the moped workforce, key organizers had more complicated backgrounds – often involving trade unions in their home countries that none of the rest of us had ever heard of.

When the Brazilian presidential elections were going on in 2018, Brazilian workers from London who had been on strike a few weeks before began sharing supportive videos of the far-right candidate Jair Bolsanaro into organizing WhatsApp chats. In the UK, they were illegal migrants involved in wildcat strikes. The far right here would, if it got its way, deport them and suppress their movement with extreme violence. But they didn't make that calculation. The contradiction between their situation in the UK and the candidate they supported in Brazil was profound.

But this kind of contradiction was precisely what we struggled to develop beyond. Because we never formed long-term organizations, we never had a chance to get everyone on the same page. There were no branch meetings to have discussions in; we rarely ended up socializing together; and our chances to chat at work varied hugely day by day. The zone centres and WhatsApp chats did a job in keeping us all in touch, but they were a very limited form of communication. The *Rebel Roo* did something to promote a common position, but it never really got the chance to go beyond arguing for strike action. Even though John McDonnel, the shadow chancellor, wrote to Deliveroo to support our demands, we had no clear relationship to the Labour party beyond their ordinary members turning up to support us at every opportunity. We were missing the chance to have deeper conversations, which would have been necessary to overcome contradictions and establish a collective political stance.

However, we did have absolute unity in action. Whenever we took to the streets, we were all part of the workers' movement on which the socialist movement relies. In the end, that practical politics outweighed whatever ideas workers might express in conversation.

UberEats

After I'd stopped working regularly for Deliveroo, UberEats started operating in the city. Their big thing was that they had an exclusive delivery agreement with McDonald's, and I saw a lot of workers with UberEats branded bags about. It seemed like it might be busy and decent money, so I gave it a go. Signing up was easy enough. They actually had a bricks-and-mortar office in Brighton which I had to go to, rather than just a storage locker. The payment structure was confusing, including a significant Uber 'fee' to be deducted for allowing you to use their platform, a boost system to increase pay at peak times, and a distance multiplier. They split the city into two zones east/west, and I lived in the east.

At first, that meant that whenever I started a shift, I got dragged much farther east, out to the Marina McDonald's. The Marina was at sea level, and every order was up into an area called Whitehawk. You had to take a narrow flyover road up and over a literal cliff to get out of the Marina, before cycling farther uphill to make the delivery. Every delivery was about a mile in total distance, but included 100 metres of vertical elevation gain. Uber's complex payment structure included increased payments for distance, but nothing for elevation, meaning that orders that took way longer were paid at a ridiculously low rate, and you were trapped into slogging your guts over a cliff for as little as £3.40 per delivery. I made £28 over 5 hours: £5.60 an hour – before costs – for totally exhausting work. The only good thing about it was the speed you picked up rolling back to the Marina to do it all again.

However, a few months later, UberEats had grown substantially. That meant there were more orders where I lived. I also realized that, if you were a bit smarter, you could strategically decline orders to avoid getting dragged away eastwards. I started working around the central McDonald's, mostly delivering from there to streets around the Level and Preston Park. The main difference between working for UberEats and working for Deliveroo was the role of McDonald's. It's no lie to say that when you're logged into UberEats you do over 50 per cent of your orders from one single restaurant. The queue to collect deliveries ended up playing the same role as the zone centre. It became an informal mass meeting point, where the design of the work process threw us together with nothing to do but talk. The other big difference was that the app allowed you to 'chain' orders, meaning that you could accept the next one before you'd delivered the one you were on. This meant that you could go drop-to-drop much more efficiently. You just kept cycling and kept swiping until you'd look up, 3 hours later, and the rush was over.

The Strikes

Being that close to a McDonald's kitchen for an extended period of time was interesting. A few UberEats riders were rude to the workers preparing orders for delivery on the other side of the counter. But, more often than not, we just felt sorry for them. You could see these despot managers giving people an earful for all sorts of menial stuff. I once saw a manager becoming increasingly incensed by the fact that a worker's sock was visible through the side of his worn-out shoe. The worker protested that he couldn't afford to buy a new pair of shoes, and, if the manager wanted him to buy some, the company should pay better wages. I thought he had a point, but the manager just kept going on and on. The pace of work in there looked frantic. The delivery counter was right in front of the station where they salted and portioned up the chips, and there was always one person whose sole job was to keep the holding rails filled with little red boxes. They'd just be standing there, taking chips out the fryer, pouring them into the big basin, covering them with salt, then using the dustpan-looking thing to fill the boxes. You'd go away and do a delivery and come back 20 minutes later, and it'd be the same person stood there, still filling boxes with chips. We cracked jokes with McDonald's workers whenever they had a moment, but that wasn't very often. I think every rider felt lucky not to be the other side of the counter.

Things worked best for everyone when the riders stuck to a strict queueing system, and the McDonalds workers just sorted things out as quickly as they could. When they were understaffed and there were loads of orders, we had to wait for a long time. That had a direct negative impact on our wages, but most riders knew whose fault it was. If McDonald's just hired enough staff to make sure there were always enough people bagging up delivery orders, then we would have been fine, but instead they often left one poor harassed person to do the work of two.

Most workers, in an attempt to get more orders at quiet times, downloaded both apps. The two companies mostly shared a workforce, and workers would swap between the two depending on which was paying better at a particular time. The two had practically identical models, with the major difference being the variable piece rate at UberEats. But, after the summer of 2018, Deliveroo introduced their own variable piece rate across the UK, which introduced the possibility that the minimum rate per drop could, on average, fall substantially below £4. Double orders were also paid at a lower rate, down from £8 to around £6. After that, the two were pretty much identical. This workforce overlap meant that for most Deliveroo/UberEats workers, the two began to seem like variants of the same boss. On any given day, you could work for one or the other. In the queue at the McDonald's delivery counter, you'd see people swapping between the two apps, being managed by two black boxes at once. That meant that, if and when future collective action occurred, it might target predominantly one platform, but both would be impacted.

By late 2017, UberEats was profitable in 27 of the 108 cities it operated in. In some places, it even significantly outperformed Uber's taxi business.[16] Dara Khosrowshahi, Uber's CEO as of 2017, has consistently increased focus on UberEats as a part of the company with the potential to deliver further growth

– particularly ahead of the first public offering of Uber shares in 2019.[17] It is in this context that rumours hit the financial press in September 2018 that Uber was in talks to buy up Deliveroo's European operation.[18] Initial speculation on price estimated that Deliveroo was worth somewhere between 2 and 4 billion dollars.[19] By buying out their biggest competitor, UberEats would become the dominant food platform in the UK and Europe. On announcement of the news, JustEat, the other big UK competitor, saw their shares fall by 7% per cent.[20]

Capitalism has, inbuilt into its mechanism, a trend towards monopolization. Big companies nearly always out-compete small companies. It's easy to assume that the centralization of economic power in the hands of a smaller and smaller group of ruling-class bosses means that workers become more and more disempowered. Historically, however, the consolidation of capital in one industry can actually increase worker leverage. The US car industry, for example, saw its largest wave of unionization immediately after a series of mergers created giants like General Motors.[21] The consolidation of the entire food-platform workforce under the management of Uber has the potential to exaggerate the already-explosive dynamic of worker resistance in the sector. It would allow one united front to be formed between tens of thousands of workers across Europe and farther afield, against one exploitative company.

This is only a speculative future, but it is towards such speculations that this book will now turn. What is going to happen to food platforms over the coming years? What is their game plan, what is the reform agenda, and what are workers going to do about it?

7

Looking Forward

As I see it, there are three perspectives on the future of food platforms. The first is the game plan of the bosses themselves. The second is that game plan modified by a liberal reform agenda. The third is some form of democratic reorganization from below, led by the workers themselves. This chapter will explore these three perspectives in turn.

Fully Automated Luxury Food Delivery?

In March 2018, a presentation given by Deliveroo to potential investors was leaked to the restaurant trade press.[1] In it, Deliveroo outlined their vision for the future. Suffice to say, it was ambitious. The company aims to double their profit margins and halve costs to customers through the full automation of food production and delivery. It's hard to tell whether this is a sincere ambition, or a fairy tale told to investors to empty their wallets and allay any panic about when they can expect a return on their investment. But, either way, their plans are worth serious consideration.

The first question is, does the tech to automate food production and delivery exist? Maybe. There are a few contending companies aiming to lead the delivery-drone field. Starship Technologies have developed drones that are essentially self-driving shopping trolleys which travel on pavements – described at sector conferences as 'under-utilised logistical infrastructure' – and fulfil short-distance deliveries within a 2-mile radius in between 5 and 30 minutes. Their position is communicated to the customer's smartphone, and they have a number of security and anti-tampering features built in. Another company working in the sector is Kiwi. They claim their robots are 65 per cent faster than standard couriers, and the company runs a fully automated delivery service at the University of California's Berkeley campus. The Kiwi model is based on the pavement drone only completing the final 300 metres of the delivery, after having been dropped off by a semi-autonomous tricycle. The most significant automated delivery pilot scheme, however, is the Amazon 'Scout' drone-delivery scheme, launched in early 2019 in Washington state.[2] The automation of simple food production is similarly being introduced in small environments. 'Flippy', a burger flipping robot, has been in operation in a number of US restaurants since early 2018, and further automation of similar simple fast-food production seems possible. However, none of these technologies has been employed on an industrial scale.

The total vision of Deliveroo indicated by these plans is a radical departure from what we know. Dark kitchens would be established in low-rent locations across a city, within something like a 2-mile radius of each other. Each of these sites, presumably only staffed by human security and engineers, would act as a production hub for their zone, with a kitchen full of robots churning out large quantities of cheap fast food on demand. A fleet of delivery drones, presumably numbering in the hundreds to cope with peak demand, would operate from the site, rolling out onto the pavement and off towards blocks of flats and basement apartments. The logistical network used by Deliveroo would be centralized and rationalized. From a decentralized mess of restaurants and customers, spread all over the map, would emerge a more regularly organized hub-and-spoke network with dark kitchens operating as distribution centres.

Powering this operation would be one of the largest and most complex databases about food delivery ever compiled. Deliveroo has collected an unprecedented dataset on the way in which we collectively eat, and each of its customers individually eats. Do we order more burgers and milkshakes on a Friday or Saturday evening? Deliveroo know, and they jealously guard this information. The platform 'locks out' restaurants from as much data as possible. In 2018, Deliveroo removed customer names and addresses from the paper receipts printed by restaurants, in order to prevent them understanding or mapping their own customer base. Deliveroo, having gained a monopoly over this data, are looking to use it as a resource to optimize their offering. What volume of food needs to be produced when, what items need to be on what menus at what times, and other business decisions can all be made with newfound precision. The potential competitive advantage is significant.

Looking Forward

The role of the Deliveroo worker would be totally transformed by this automation, of course. Chefs, software engineers, and couriers are all at risk of being tossed onto the scrapheap if Deliveroo's utopia is realized. Many of them would end up becoming trapped in crippling debt, unemployment, and poverty – particularly couriers, laid off without any of the claims to redundancy afforded to employees. A glorious new world of on-demand food delivery awaits us.

But would it really work? There are a number of obvious impediments to this model. First and foremost is a question of investment: would Deliveroo be able to raise the capital to invest in a global network of dark kitchens, complex robots, security staff, mechanics, additional software engineers, and the like before the platform capitalism bubble pops? They've still never turned an annual profit, and if there is a global economic downturn in the interim between this dream entering CEO Will Shu's head and its actual execution, the massive surplus capital investment which makes the Deliveroo model possible might vanish.

Beyond that, there are all kinds of technical questions to be answered. Could a small city like Brighton handle 500+ delivery drones on its pavements? How would these drones interact with human and vehicle traffic on a mass scale? What would rates of theft be like? How would the government regulate them? Whenever I describe this potential future of automated shopping trollies rolling around our pavements, I always get the same response: won't drunk people just sabotage the whole thing? It's not hard to imagine the many possible ways drunk people could mess with delivery drones: riding on the back of them, trapping them in someone's

143

garden, and throwing them in the sea all figure highly on the list. If human Deliveroo drivers already get harassed working on a Saturday night, it seems likely that Deliveroo drones would be the subject of even more negative attention.

In terms of food production, Deliveroo's menu of automated options might have to be restricted to burgers and chips, with human food preparation being retained for anything more complex. And beyond the small details, it's not at all obvious that Deliveroo has the experience to handle the challenges they would face whilst transitioning from an agile and expansive platform with limited investment in fixed capital to a company committed to owning, maintaining, and securing huge quantities of property and machinery.

Beyond these technical and change-management questions are the political questions of any such transition. When workers with relatively little to lose see their livelihoods being phased out, they can become very militant, very fast. The early industrial revolution saw craft weavers threatened with poverty by the development of mechanized textile mills launch a mass campaign of machine-breaking. They were named 'Luddites' after the movement's fictional leader, Ned Ludd. Could the phase-out of Deliveroo couriers take place without Luddite-style mass machine-breaking of delivery drones? In San Francisco, Starship drones have already been roughed up by pedestrians, and that's without hundreds of angry, unemployed ex-Deliveroo workers sitting around with nothing to do.[3] Platform capitalism is already flammable – the issue of automation might prompt an inferno.

All considered, the barriers to the development of Deliveroo into a profitable and highly automated drone-based delivery company are significant. Whatever the future of the company is going to be, it is not going to be what the bosses think it is.

Progressive Futurism

For those who see this future of mass unemployment of food delivery drivers as potentially a bad thing, Tim O'Reilly, Silicon Valley venture capitalist and CEO, has a solution. O'Reilly is a progressive liberal, who acknowledges that the latest stage of capitalism is getting out of hand. Workers aren't being treated right, and the rich are getting too rich. He wants to 'play the game of business as if people matter'.[4] To work out how to do that, O'Reilly variously cites Jonathan Hall (an economist at Uber), Professor Andrei Haigu (in the *Harvard Business Review*), Simon Rothmans (venture capitalist), Tom Perez (secretary of labor under Obama), Steven Hill (of the Google-backed New America think tank), and Jose Alvarez (ex-CEO). His positive examples of social change are those luminaries of human emancipation, Mark Zuckerberg and Elon Musk.[5] His argument represents, in short, the ideas of the bleeding-heart ruling class.

His analysis of working conditions at a global platform like Uber begins with a very specific element of US employment law: that when employees work for over 30 hours a week, employers have a responsibility to pay a full-time benefits package. As a result, companies like Walmart and McDonald's maintain huge workforces on 29-hour-a-week schedules, with rotas organized via automated scheduling processes. This intentionally leaves employees in an unprotected grey area. The obvious solution to this, of course, is that every employer – be they outsourcing company or multinational giant – has to pay a full array of benefits to every worker, regardless of hours worked. In the US context, an even more obvious development would be for access to healthcare to be guaranteed – free at the point of use to everyone through a national health service. Then, there would be no need for workers to be slavishly reliant on an employer in order to get access to healthcare.

But no, O'Reilly has a different idea. His reform agenda begins from the idea that the solution to this benefits problem is to make all companies *more like platforms*. His argument goes as follows: Uber workers can work as many hours as they want. Therefore, they are better off than Walmart workers trapped on 29 hours a week. So, working for Uber is better than working for Walmart – and so all employment should be reorganized along platform lines. Of course, Uber doesn't pay a comprehensive benefits package at all, and its workers have no guaranteed minimum rate of pay that means they will earn more than the Walmart worker after costs – but this escapes his analysis.

O'Reilly's initial premise is that, at the moment, capitalism operates as if its human workers are disposable things. He identifies that our social system is based only on the maximization of profit, rather than what's best for the majority of the population. To his credit, he does think this is a problem. But, despite starting from this recognition, his blundering argument fails to reach the most obvious conclusions. He can't see that the exploitation of labour is hardwired into the basic logic of capitalism, or that technological development under this

146

is dictated by the interests of a tiny class dictatorship of billionaires. He won't admit that the entire 'game of business' is based on the domination of one class by another, and needs to be dumped unceremoniously into the dustbin of history, alongside feudalism, slavery, and all the other relics of a darker past. He knows that workers' lives are being 'crushed in the machine' – but refuses to go any further than shrugging his shoulders when asked what the machine is, how it works, and how we smash it. All that is clear is that he thinks that making the lives of Walmart workers more like the lives of Uber workers will help. But exploitation is no historical hiccup that we can reform our way around – it's the basic condition of capitalist society. Austerity in the UK alone has led to 120,000 excess deaths since 2010.[6] In the context of a class war from above as vacuous as this, politics becomes polarized. O'Reilly, it seems, has picked a side – and it's not ours.

Progressive liberalism has no answers to the problems posed by the exploitation of labour under platform capitalism – because it has never had an answer to capitalism at all. There are no new ideas here, apart from a desperate plea to everyone to be nice to each other. O'Reilly's critique of socialism is that a total top-to-bottom transformation of the social relations of capitalism inevitably leads to disaster. No, instead, he argues, we have to go with the system we have, and try to modify it to make it nicer. The way to avoid disaster is to double down on a commitment to a social system that is currently a few decades of fossil-fuel emissions away from ending the possibility of human life on earth. *That* is how we can make everything better. It's hardly a convincing argument.

It is obvious that workers cannot rely on venture capitalists and charitable billionaires to solve the crises we face. Our answer has to be based in something more than progressive futurist hand-waving. The working class has to free itself through its own struggle.

Platform Cooperativism or Workers' Control?

Food platforms are locked in a cut-throat battle for supremacy. Deliveroo, UberEats, Foodora, JustEat, Glovo, Wolt, Caviar – the list is endless. In Amsterdam alone, there have been periods in the past two years when seven different food-delivery services have been operating at once. Each platform wants to win as much market share as possible, and is willing to provide services at a serious loss if it increases their market share and starves out competitors. All of these firms rely on vast sums of venture capital, which allow them to absorb big losses in pursuit of dominance.

It is in this context that some reformers like Trebor Scholz, to the left of the progressive liberalism of Tim O'Reilly, have begun to focus in on the idea of platform cooperatives. A simplified version of the idea is as follows: there is a large pool of dissatisfied workers and conscientious customers connected via these platforms. By connecting these workers (both couriers and software engineers) with these customers via a new cooperative platform structure, the dominance of existing private platforms could be challenged. These competing cooperatives could offer better working conditions and offer workers and consumers a greater degree of control. Because workers already provide the means of subsist-

148

ence for the existing private platforms, the app is the only fixed capital required to get a co-op going. Entering the food-platform market as a cooperative is comparatively easy compared to other sectors, given the lower start-up costs and the lightweight business model. Sometimes, co-op enthusiasts overestimate the ease of developing a Deliveroo-esque app, but the basic argument holds water. The problems of platform cooperativism are not in this sequence of conclusions, but rather in the actual details of what happens once a cooperative has entered the market.

If a successful large-scale cooperative food-delivery platform was established, it would immediately become the focus of an onslaught by the dominant capitalist platforms. This would likely consist of a two-pronged attack: first, a massive investment in lobbying and misinformation to undermine popular support for the cooperative; and, second, an aggressive competition strategy offering higher wages to lure away workers, and lower prices to lure away customers. The dominant private platforms, enabled by venture capital, already run at a significant loss in many of their locations in an effort to undermine competitors. Given that a co-op could not call on similar cash reserves, it's hard to see how it could compete. The results of this twofold pressure might well produce effects that undermine the whole purpose of a cooperative. In order to try to protect the market share of their cooperative, workers would likely accept lower wages, and so get locked into an intractable race to the bottom they were supposed to have escaped. Self-exploitation, not much different from the effects of a piece wage, would be the condition of viability. So, this is the first sticking point of platform cooperativism: on an economic level, it takes no account of competitive pressure. Given that food platforms are already running each other into the ground to dominate a market with no clear profit margins, the opportunities for the development of large co-op competitors seem limited.[7]

One strategy with extensive historical precedent that might be used to prevent a platform co-op going under in the face of a venture capital-funded onslaught would be an equally aggressive strategy of state intervention. This intervention would have to find a mechanism to prevent the existing dominant platforms from undermining co-ops. It's likely that the only way to do so would be to restrict the vast resources of the dominant platforms via licensing, regulation, or some other measure, in order to create space in the market for self-managed platform cooperatives to grow.

Given this, one might well ask whether cooperatives made possible by state-level action and the regulation of platforms would really only consist of a poor version of a more expansive politics of workers' control. If the political will exists to restrict the operation of large platforms, why not also progressively undermine the private ownership of their assets and develop democratic mechanisms for their control from below? Rather than platform cooperativism combined with technocratic state restriction of competition, we could imagine a more ambitious alternative: platform expropriation under workers' control.

Platform expropriation would consist of workers taking ownership of the private resources of food platforms – such as their data centres, dark kitchens, and customer base. This would be a mild form of reparation for all the profit made by Will Shu, Dan Warne, and others off the back of exploited workers. This expropriated capital would then be placed under workers' control via a system of democratic self-management participated in by all workers, from office cleaners to software engineers, call centre staff, app watchers, and delivery riders.

The resulting food platform, a people's Deliveroo, would not be run in the interests of bosses and their profits. Instead, its end goal would be to provide a socially useful service. Workers' control would likely lead to an internal revolution in the way that this service is provided, and the platform operates. The abolition of piece wages, and the transparent redesign of the app from a black-box algorithmic manager to a democratically controlled algorithmic planner, both seem like obvious first steps. However, to really grasp the potential of this radical programme of transformation, the platform needs to be understood from the perspective of both the worker in the platform and the worker that uses the platform. The Lucas plan is an often-cited example of how workers can come up with ideas for the redevelopment of their industries to produce for social need under workers' control. Lucas Aerospace workers created the plan in the 1970s in an attempt to stave off layoffs. They proposed a series of socially useful technologies which the company could produce, in the place of the existing technology made by the firm.[8]

What might the Deliveroo/UberEats plan look like? The context for such a development could be an expanding provision of universal basic services (UBS). The UBS idea recently gained prominence via a 2017 UCL Institute for Global Prosperity report.[9] The report argued for the introduction of a range of services, free at the point of access, covering healthcare, education, democracy and legal services, shelter, transport, information, and food. One of the options envisioned in the discussion of a universal basic food service was a 'full community food programme'. This programme is described by the authors as follows:

> A community service with completely open access for all ... This option embodies the kind of social institutional fabric that would support and develop a truly cohesive society in which UBS provide shared experiences and communal environments. ... A community food program would necessarily be locally designed and delivered and would include many varieties of food service in every locality, from public canteens to food boxes for in-home preparation. Different options would cater for different dietary preferences (e.g. vegetarian) and different modalities (e.g. take away or eat in). Some communities might offer more options and others less, all of which would be decided by, and managed by, an accountable local democracy. This option would have a total cost of around £21.2Bn, with values to households ranging from £45/week in the lowest deciles to £1.63/week in the highest deciles. Our cursory distributional analysis assumes lower take up rates in higher deciles, with 5% of those in the highest decile only using the service for 0.5 meals/week, while those in the lowest deciles would use 14 meals/week.[10]

An on-demand delivery platform under workers' control is an obvious candidate for part of the 'social institutional fabric' that this kind of programme would rely upon. A certain number of deliveries a week could be offered as part of the state pension, as part of maternity and paternity leave, as part of disability support allowance, and on NHS prescription for outpatients. A platform-based worker-run 'meals on wheels' service could begin to provide for the needs of an ageing population and expand the support available to those with additional temporary or permanent care needs. Additional on-demand delivery functions could be connected to a renationalized Royal Mail, with couriers providing another final-stage logistical option.

Dark kitchen sites could be turned into community food infrastructure in line with the wider UBS vision. Collective kitchens could be run by the community and provide a multitude of social goods. They could use their procurement power to support the development of workers' control in agriculture. A high-wage apprentice system could provide food preparation skills to young people, and excess menial labour could be strategically reduced through the use of technology. These sites could be expanded from just delivery kitchens to fulfil the functions of restaurants and pubs, developing community cohesion through infrastructure that is redesigned for human need and not for profit. In some cases, they could be relocated closer to existing community hubs via the expropriation of under-used or empty commercial property. Community provision of food has always been an integral part of how human beings look after each other – this new vision would only be an extension of that fundamental solidarity through modern technological means.

The possibilities of a People's Deliveroo are limited only by our capacity to image a better society. Marx famously refused to write cookbooks for the chefs of the future, by which he meant he wouldn't predict the exact form in which socialism would emerge in advance. But perhaps it's possible to speculate about how those future cooks will get their food from kitchen to table.

The Question of Power

Speculations about platform expropriation under workers' control remain completely utopian if they do not deal with the question of power. The ruling class have no interest in allowing workers to own and run the organizations they work for. That kind of reorganization of society from the bottom up will only be possible if the working class overturn the dominance of their bosses through class struggle. To understand the depth of the challenges which spiral out from that kind of confrontation, we have to address the relationship between democracy and capitalism.

Though the mainstream opinion is that capitalism and democracy have always gone hand in hand, the reality is more uncomfortable. Liberalism (understood as the political ideology of the capitalist ruling class) has had to mediate between these two potentially contradictory systems for centuries. Historian Ishay Landa argues that early liberals were fundamentally opposed to democracy. Thinkers like Locke and Burke were committed to the first principle of capitalism, private property, not the first principle of democracy: all the power to all the people.[11] Liberals only grudgingly accepted giving ordinary people the right to vote when the socialist movement forced their hand.[12] Democracy would be tolerated – however, this tolerance had a limit. This limit was private property. Democratic control of 'politics' was fine (that wasn't where the power was, anyway). But democratic control of the economy was beyond the pale.

Landa proposes that, whenever this limit has been challenged, liberalism has historically undergone a split: liberals who prioritize its political commitments to democracy have tended to side with forces on the left, whereas the (majority of) liberals who prioritize private property and capitalism have had to look for other allies against the working class. Historically, these allies have been fascists. The sensible support of sensible members of the ruling class for the 'unfortunately necessary'[13] dictatorial regimes which prevent workers taking control of the economy itself – be they headed by Mussolini, Pinochet, or Bolsanaro – is the result of the contradictory limits of capitalist democracy and the failures of its ruling political ideology, liberalism.

So, the political stakes underlying the proposals of expropriation under workers' control should not be underestimated. Breaking the grip of the ruling class on the means of production is not a problem that can be skipped around with smart policy and branding. If workers get their hands on the levers of society and begin to challenge the fundamental basis of the mode of production, a desperate fight ensues between extreme reactionaries and the forces of social transformation. Examples of what this struggle looks like are scattered across the last century: Spain 1936, Chile 1973, Greece 2015, and many more besides. A people's Deliveroo might sound like common sense, but to achieve it alongside the more general transition to a socialist society, the workers' movement would have to be able to defeat the ruling class and its allies by exerting more power than them. It's not enough to have a majority in parliament, because, in the final instance, the ruling class don't care about democracy – they care about ruling. The future of platforms will be determined by the balance of power between classes.

8

A New Wave

Two years on from the strike that started it all, another strike broke out in London. This time, the primary target was UberEats, not Deliveroo – although almost all the couriers involved worked for both. The strike began when UberEats changed its pay structure, notionally lowering the minimum fee per drop from £4.26 to £3.50. Because of a further change in the calculation of deliveries, workers were actually getting paid below even this minimum. They started seeing deliveries for as little as £2.60 – a 40 per cent pay cut.

On the first day of the strike, WhatsApp messages flashed across London, spreading the news of the action to different areas. One video in particular went viral, being forwarded from group to group. It showed a worker standing outside a McDonald's, speaking in Brazilian Portuguese, explaining to the camera that him and his mates would make sure that no orders went out from there all day. The strike was on. Picket lines were set up outside McDonald's restaurants all over the city. When scabs tried to break the strike, things got heated. I heard a story of pickets locking up the bike of one scabbing worker to stop him working as he tried to force his way inside to pick up a delivery. He left, defeated, only to come back to break up the picket line with a group of mates and a knife. Bit by bit, the whole complex system began to grind to a halt. Later in the day, a demonstration was organized, and over 200 workers converged at the Uber Greenlighting centre in Aldgate, East London. They demanded £5 a drop, and tried to force the Uber bosses to negotiate with them directly. A leaflet handed out across London called for another demonstration the next day.

So, on day two of the strike, 20 September, I found myself and fifty workers gathering in a side street near Aldgate Station. It was still a half-hour until the demonstration was due to start, and everyone was standing around in little groups. Every few minutes another group of five or ten workers would arrive from some distant part of zone 3 or 4, blasting their horns and cheering. I started talking to workers about the situation, and why they had decided to go on strike. The stories were upsetting. One rider was working over 60 hours a week, and still had to borrow money off his family to pay his rent. Slowly, the crowd grew. The police gave up on their attempts to keep the road clear. Security guards were brought out to control the Uber office entrances. Curious office workers on their lunch break started to form a crowd on a set of steps nearby. Chants started to bounce off the surrounding buildings. At first, it was only a meek 'Two pound sixty, shame on you'. But before long the workers found their voice, and the slogan that would dominate the rest of the day: 'No money, no food!' More workers arrived, in bigger groups now. Some were on video chat with workers at picket lines elsewhere, showing them how big the demonstration was getting. It was the largest UberEats strike ever, by some distance. The trade unionists from the IWGB and IWW, who'd shown up to support the workers, were inundated with questions. Small huddles formed around them, with workers asking a few variants of one question: could the union force the bosses to negotiate?

A low-level manager came out the front of the building and reaffirmed the company's stance that Uber would only talk to riders one-on-one, after having verified the details of their account. He handed out a letter offering a minimum-payment guarantee of £9–£11 per hour (pre-costs) and explaining that 'our door is always open for individual couriers to speak to us' – the workers literally ripped it up. Organic leaders emerged out of the crowd and started to formulate demands and articulate the strikers' case. When that failed, a huddle at the head of the crowd began to lead a mass meeting, which decided to demand four things: £5 a drop, £1 extra per mile, an end to the boost system, and no victimizations. An idea began to circulate: 'the bosses need to come out here and speak to us to resolve this problem', one worker said, 'otherwise we're going to go to Piccadilly Circus, 300 bikes up, and stop London from working. Buses, businesses, stopped!' A splinter group, growing bored of the meeting, went back up to the Uber manager and surrounded him. One worker stepped forward to lead a new interrogation: 'Would you do deliveries in your car for £2.50? Listen, I've been almost robbed twice . . .'. Then, from the crowd behind, came that chant again – 'No money, no food'. The manager turned, slipped past two security guards, and retreated behind big glass doors. 'He's run away!' It all felt a bit familiar.

This signalled the end of the attempt to force a negotiation at this office. Now, the workers set off in a huge flying picket. They were heading to Aldgate Tower, home to Uber's high-level management offices. When they arrived, they pulled up in the major junction where Whitechapel High Street meets Commercial Street, just up from Altab Ali Park. Traffic was blocked almost immediately. Workers spilled over onto the pavement, parking their mopeds and then surging up to the giant glass front doors of the building. They waved printed A4 signs in broken English: 'Say NO to Uber greed to cut our income'. By now, the whole tower was on lockdown. The police arrived and attempted to clear the junction. At first, it was just one car, trying to force a removals van through the blockade. The lone, beleaguered police officer who got out to clear the crowd was confronted by thirty workers telling him there was no way the van was getting through. He got the message, ran back to his car, and waited for back-up. Fifteen minutes later, enough police officers arrived to clear half the junction, and then after another ten minutes, the full junction. Workers held speeches on the steps by the front doors. Henry Chango Lopez, president of the IWGB, addressed the crowd, and argued that workers needed to join a union to keep the organizing going. At 3.20 p.m., a senior police officer decided to impose conditions on the demonstration: the UberEats workers would have to move on by 4 p.m., or they would face arrest. The human right to withdraw your labour did not apply outside the Uber office, by order of the Metropolitan Police. The workers responded to the threat by continuing the flying picket elsewhere, at Parliament Square.

The London strike had been foreshadowed by smaller strikes over the summer in Southampton, Plymouth, Glasgow, and Cardiff, all of which had taken place in response to low 'boost' rates and the resulting low piece rate. Pressure was building across the country, and this London strike was only the biggest expression of a wider anger.

Everywhere, October 2018

After the London strike, the flame caught. For the first time, rather than one city striking in isolation, the strike was spreading. Not over the course of weeks or months, but hours. On the morning after the demonstration at Uber HQ, workers in Plymouth stayed in bed. They didn't set up a picket line or hold a demonstration, they all just had a coordinated day off. In a small city like that, it was possible for the workers to be so well networked that they didn't need a picket line. They just played video games at home whilst one restaurant after another turned the app off and the service ground to a halt. By 8.30 a.m., UberEats was already sending out boost texts: 'complete 3 deliveries accepted between 9am and 11am to receive £10 on top of your usual fares'. But the strike held. Back in London, Saturday saw another, smaller demonstration. Friends who worked at McDonald's in South London told me that orders were still piling up on the counter. The pitched battle of Thursday was giving way to a kind of guerrilla warfare.

At the same time as hundreds of strikers had been besieging the Uber office in Aldgate, the Bakers, Food and Allied Workers Union (BFAWU) and Unite had announced coordinated strike action for 4 October. Workers at ten McDonald's, Wetherspoons, and TGI Fridays sites were going to walk out. A group of striking Wetherspoons workers wrote that:

> It can be hard to live on the money we make. We spend most of our wages on renting damp flats, we have to walk to work when we can't afford the bus, and we have to choose between dinner and a haircut. We're forced to work as fast as we can for long shifts with barely any breaks, even when we're sick or injured. We've seen the people we work with struggling to make ends meet, sofa surfing and scraping by.
>
> Meanwhile, Tim Martin is worth £322 million. Our work has made him, the bosses, and the shareholders rich beyond our wildest dreams, but we're left a few weeks' pay away from poverty.
>
> We won't take it anymore. That's why we're fighting back. They won't listen to us when we complain, so we're taking the next step. In two Brighton pubs we've taken the decision to all stop work and go on strike on October 4th. We're fighting for £10 an hour and union recognition for every Wetherspoons worker in the country.
>
> On your own, you can't change anything. Hiding in the freezer, stretching out your break time, getting another job – none of it solves the problem. The bosses have all the power and they don't give a shit about us. We know that we will only win when we fight together.[1]

162

That sense, that 'we will only win when we fight together', was even more widespread than it first appeared. Two strike movements had emerged in two supposedly unorganizable areas: precarious hospitality work, and precarious food-platform work. The crossover soon began to be solidified into practical cooperation.

On May Day 2018, International Workers' Day, McDonald's workers in the UK had taken part in the second #McStrike. Workers at five stores walked out demanding better wages, conditions, and contracts. The strike was, on its own merit, an example of how precarious service workers can organize. But there was another specific development. The IWW Couriers Network released a solidarity statement with the McStrike. Now, in a way, this in unsurprising – workers support other workers all the time. It's called a workers' movement for a reason. But what really matters is that UberEats does a huge proportion of its deliveries from McDonald's, meaning that this kind of solidarity had within it the embryonic possibility for an industrial alliance between food-delivery and food-preparation workers.

Cooperation began with a group chat. Key organizers from a few different unions came together to discuss how this momentum could be converted into joint strike action. Before long, there were five unions involved in some capacity: BFAWU, Unite, GMB, IWW, IWGB. They were a mix of all kinds of union: from the biggest trade union in the country and mainstays of the Trade Union Congress, to the syndicalist IWW and the young grassroots union the IWGB. They began to discuss how to broaden and circulate the strike. The fact that employment law didn't apply to platform workers meant that they could be flexible with their strike timeline, so the unions representing them agreed to make a concerted effort to take action on 4 October. Before long, the first ever national courier strike was called by the IWW Couriers Network. It was going to be the biggest food-platform strike ever, across seven cities, with solidarity action in seven more.

Solidarity strikes, which had been one of the strongest weapons of the working-class movement until they were made illegal by the Thatcher government of 1980, were suddenly a legitimate possibility. Plans were made for mass secondary picketing – where workers from one company picket the workplace of another. In this case, UberEats workers would picket McDonald's both to prevent orders being picked up and to support the workers inside. Different groups of workers at different points in the supply chain would be actively combining their efforts to increase their combined leverage. The upcoming strike gained significant political support when Momentum, the Corbyn-supporting faction within the Labour party, asked their local groups to organize solidarity actions and community pickets on the day. An article written by Wetherspoons workers ahead of their strike ended with the line: 'there are tens of thousands of us and only a few of them – together, we can run our pubs for the many not the few', echoing both the Labour party slogan and the idea of workers' control of the means of production. The movement was developing, fast.

As midnight approached on 3 October, workers' in the Post and Telegraph (one of the Wetherspoons pubs in Brighton) prepared to walk out. A group of managers had assembled by one end of the bar, waiting nervously to see how many staff would leave as the strike day began. A few seconds after midnight, the walk-out began. A crowd of about fifty supporters and other strikers met the strikers at the door. Their first chant was: 'I believe that we will win.' The crowd marched over to a second striking pub, to do the same thing there. Behind the workers, a group of drunk young men started chanting too: 'E, E, EDL'. It was easy to forget at times, but far-right street movements were providing their own response to the crisis – one that targeted Muslims and let the ruling class off the hook. Other students, likely freshers enjoying their first month at university, shouted their drunken support. The strike was on. The fast-food shutdown had begun.

Things got started in London at 8 a.m. with a picket of Brixton McDonald's. A demonstration in Kentish Town took place during the morning rush hour, as people were heading into work. At 11 a.m., Leicester Square played host to 300 workers and supporters from Wetherspoons, McDonald's, and TGIs. The shadow chancellor John McDonnell addressed the strikers: 'The message to every exploitative employer in this country is that we're coming for you. We're not tolerating low pay, insecurity or lack of respect. We will mobilize as one movement, the Labour and trade union movement, in solidarity. And I guarantee you this: with strength, determination, courage, and solidarity, we will win.' At the same time, a picket called by Momentum was taking place outside a Wetherspoons in Chester.

At midday, the first of two demonstrations to be held in the city that day began in Glasgow's George Square. Similar rallies took place at the same time in Newcastle, Sheffield, and Wrexham. In Cambridge, a group of supporters held a community picket of a striking McDonald's. Their slogan was 'McStrike to Win'.

At 1 p.m., a group of thirty Uber drivers, couriers, and supporters organized by the IWGB and IWW went to demonstrate at Uber HQ in Aldgate Tower. A few weeks beforehand, a huge strike demonstration had been locked outside. This time, however, they kept a low profile and snuck through the doors. As soon as they were inside, the banners, flags, and megaphones were out. For forty-five minutes, they occupied the reception, chanting: 'Mr Boss, you must listen, we'll shut down your algorithm!' A French food-platform worker from the Collectif des Livreurs Autonomes de Paris (the Paris Autonomous Deliverers' Collective: CLAP), who had travelled to the UK to support the strike, relayed everything that was happening to workers in France. Building security ran backwards and forwards, looking flustered but unable to do anything to control the situation. The riders were refusing to be hidden behind the black box any longer.

However, the riders had yet to seriously enter the fight. That would change over the next few hours. At 5 p.m., their first ever national strike began. The strength of the action varied widely city by city, but in Cardiff, Bristol, Glasgow, and London, enough workers managed to get together to make a serious impact. Footage from the strikes in Bristol showed a huge flying picket – probably up there with the biggest ever formed outside of London. Before the picket set off, a migrant worker gave a speech:

> There is, like you guys know, loads of people above us planning to make the fee drop go down and make it worse for everyone. That's what we don't want. That's why we have to be here together and fight together. For that reason, everyone, we have a strike together, we're

going to show them we have force – force to ask for what is fair, for everyone that's working for Uber and Deliveroo.

The London strike demonstration didn't grow to the size it had done a few weeks beforehand, but on a local level the strike held. Riders were logging off and going home, rather than going to East London.[2] At the same time, demonstrations and community pickets were held in Birmingham, Bradford, Leeds, Camden, Manchester, and Swansea. For the first time, action was widespread, coordinated, and closely integrated into a larger political narrative.

The final action of the day took place back in Brighton. A strike rally of 300 people in support of the Wetherspoons workers gathered in the centre of town at 6.30 p.m. Contingents from the National Union of Journalists (NUJ), Universities and Colleges Union (UCU), GMB, and Labour party were all there. Striking workers spoke to the crowd about their action and the conditions they faced. Every time a speaker mentioned the Brighton community, they got a huge cheer. At the end of the rally, a local musician played a song he'd written for the strikers: 'We'll call last orders tonight, and then we're all going out on strike.' The crowd began to sing along with the chorus.

The crowd split in half and went to picket the two pubs. The pickets were noisy, with workers and supporters spilling over from the pavements, and massing in front of the doors. At the Post and Telegraph, two police officers were brought in to personally escort any customers who wanted to undermine the strike across the picket line. Only a few suited men took them up on the offer. The chants kept on coming: 'Shut it down, shut it down, Brighton is a union town.' The windows of the pub were significantly above ground level, so it was hard to see inside, but some pickets who climbed on top of bins reported that it looked almost empty. After a few hours, the picket ended. When it came time for some of the strikers to go back in for the last hours of their shifts (which ran after midnight into 5 October), both pubs had been closed early. The pub managers informed the returning strikers that they would be getting paid for the rest of their shift anyway.

Four days later, the CLAP rider who'd stood in the Uber offices alongside UberEats workers was part of a strike back in Paris against pay cuts. Workers gathered in groups at their zone centres – twenty in Montparnasse, ten in the west, fifty in the north. They then rode en masse to the Place de la République. The coming weeks would see French riders storming Deliveroo's office and mounting blockades of dark kitchen sites.

Five days later, on 9 October, Uber taxi drivers, organized with the UPHD, called their first national strike. Rallies were called outside three offices in London, Birmingham, and Nottingham. The circulation of struggle didn't let up. Their demands were: £2 a mile (up from £1.25), 10 per cent reduction in the Uber commission to 15 per cent, an end to unfair dismissals, and to be legally defined as self-employed workers not independent contractors. Yaseem Aslam, a minicab driver with the IWGB, said in the days beforehand that 'he had never seen workers uniting like this'. Three years of patient organizing efforts by the union were about to be tested.

Their demonstration in London was to be outside Aldgate Tower again. For the fourth time in a month, Uber's offices would be a target. Over 200 drivers turned up. They tried to get into the lobby, only to be aggressively pushed back by the police. Italian drivers started singing the famous anti-fascist partisan song, *Bella Ciao*. An IWW courier who'd travelled all the way from Cardiff to show his solidarity was on the megaphone leading chants.

On 26 October, food-platform workers from thirty-five unions/collectives and twelve states met in Brussels to form the Transnational Courier Federation. The struggle continues.

The Network Model

How did the IWW come to be the major union behind the first national food-platform strike? It's an interesting question. Initially, they were involved in two smaller local struggles in Bristol and Leeds, but the first major national wave of action mostly passed them by. In response, they developed what they call 'the network model'.

This network model is based on their prior experience of failure. Its pioneers were the Cardiff IWW branch. Cardiff IWW had attempted to participate in the national 'Roovolution' organizing drive alongside IWW branches in Leeds and Bristol in 2017. This drive failed. They didn't organize a sustainable union branch, and no strikes or protests developed out of their agitating. But that failure provided the local branch with two things: first, they now understood what did not work;

and, second, they had recruited a couple of full-time couriers who would be the basis for future organizing efforts.

Their second attempt began to develop the network model, and was premised on a new understanding of the necessary modifications of classical union organizing that need to be made in order to suit it to the context of Deliveroo and other food-delivery platforms. It had significantly more local success as a result, and developed an organizing methodology that was ready for national roll-out the next time significant momentum developed.

The strategy of this network model is dictated by a process of workers' inquiry. Previous attempts to agitate specifically around legal status in 2017 had proved fruitless because they didn't resonate with workers. As one branch member put it:

> We went back to kind of basic organising 101: get some people in a room, and ask 'what are you actually pissed off about, what are your actual problems?' We focused purely on getting the riders to collectively start to take action, rather than us going in with an agenda saying: 'you should be worried about workers' rights', and then they say: 'well, we're not at the moment'. There were obviously one or two who were, but the majority were like 'pfft, what we really worry about is the fact that we're waiting half hour/forty-five minutes at McDonalds or Wagamama's', or the fact that managers at restaurants treated them like crap. It was those day-to-day conditions of labour that were more in the forefront, because they saw them as one of the main reasons why they weren't able to do enough orders to make enough money.

This inquiry highlighted what kind of issues workers would be willing to fight over. Everyday issues like waiting times would be prioritized over employment rights, for the time being at least. Now they had some initial answers, the branch focused on creating an organizational structure which would suit food-platform workers specifically. In practice, this means a network model with three layers. On the outside is the courier network itself. This is a WhatsApp group, comprised of a broad collection of more or less organized workers in both Deliveroo and UberEats, given that the two platforms basically share a workforce. This layer is the mass base for the organizing drive and any subsequent collective action. Below that is a core of 'courier members' – that is, union members who work as full-time couriers. Their only job is to agitate amongst the workforce, identify and recruit organic leaders,[3] and constantly expand the network in an effort to neutralize the impact of rapid workforce turnover. Below that again is the general branch membership. These union members don't work as couriers but help the campaign by doing essential support work such as logistics, administration, representation, and communication. These general members provide the structure for the network from outside, and act as reinforcements wherever necessary. Because of the way the IWW is structured, they are all unpaid volunteers, rather than full-time officials.

The initial impact of the model was to organize a consistent fight to take chunks out of the platforms from below. During their inquiry, the Cardiff network identified that waiting times and bad treatment at McDonald's were a serious problem for UberEats couriers. So, they began to organize low-level collective action. The network wrote letters to McDonald's both locally and nationally, as well as to UberEats

HQ, demanding action. When they were stonewalled, the general members of the union attended the stores to follow up. The general membership represented the workers like this in order to avoid couriers being identified and victimized. They were told their problems had been passed on to head office. UberEats refused to meet with the network, and instead sent down representatives to circumnavigate the network entirely and speak to individual riders. This attempt at indirect negotiation seems to have three intentions: to delegitimize the network, to diffuse the tension, and to split the workforce. However, this attempt to break the union failed. As a result, the network began to build a substantial power base within the workforce.

Other IWW branches took up the idea, and, by the time of the October strike, the courier network had either sympathetic contacts or fully established branches in five Scottish cities (Glasgow, Edinburgh, Aberdeen, Stirling, and Inverness), thirteen English cities (London, Bristol, Manchester, Cambridge, Leicester, Birmingham, Plymouth, Southampton, Manchester, Bradford, Leeds, Sheffield, and York), four Welsh cities (Cardiff, Newport, Swansea, and Aberystwyth), and four Irish cities (Derry, Belfast, Dublin, Cork). In London, in particular, a network of supporters came together to systematically contact workers outside almost every McDonald's in the city before the strike. They distributed over 10,000 multi-lingual flyers.

The courier network model has been developed by the IWW through workers' inquiry. It is deliberately adapted to the specific conditions of worker resistance within platform capitalism, and as a result it seems to be working. For the first time, long-term organization seems to be replacing short-term mobilization. This is the most significant development in the patterns of worker resistance in the UK since 2016, and could potentially indicate that, this time round, food-platform worker self-organization has serious staying power.

9

Conclusion

When you understand a workplace from the workers' point of view, all kinds of previously invisible phenomena come into view. Deliveroo – which looks on the surface like the shiny model of a new economy – is revealed to be based on a class composition that's prone to explosions of struggle. An atomized workforce of hundreds of couriers spread across a city are revealed to be organized through a tight-knit invisible structure that allows them to take mass coordinated action. Cities across the world are revealed to be linked by a transnational strike wave which has been building and building for the last two years. Below the turquoise and sushi exterior, food platforms are laboratories of class struggle.

Why laboratories? Italian workerist Raniero Panzieri, reflecting on the role of technology in capitalism (with particular reference to the FIAT car manufacturing plants of northern Italy), argued that: 'the subversive strength of the working class, its revolutionary capacity, appears (potentially) strongest precisely at capitalism's "development points", where the crushing preponder-

174

Conclusion

ance of constant capital over living labour, together with the rationality embodied in the former, immediately faces the working class with the question of its political enslavement'.[1] Where the ruling class has developed new forms of capital (such as an algorithmic management system) that expresses the total political domination of bosses over workers (such as the rationality embedded in a black box), the political questions of the class struggle are posed more acutely – and workers respond more acutely as a result. Panzieri might have been talking about car manufacturing but his insights apply just as well to the development of food platforms.

The experience of work at Deliveroo is organized through a system of control based on the use of a black-box algorithmic manager and a piece rate payment structure (which is only possible because of the use of independent contractor legal status). This system of control uses precarity to increase the rate of exploitation, but even precarious workers can self-organize. The labour process results in an underlying tendency towards the creation of organic solidarities through encrypted messenger chat groups and physical meetings, although these are not always guaranteed. When taken together, these solidarities are the invisible organization out of which collective worker resistance can emerge.

The workers at Deliveroo, particularly in Brighton, are divided into two camps – both under pressure due to high rents, low wages, and a competitive unskilled labour market. Workers on mopeds do the bulk of the work and are often migrants with significant financial commitments. On the other hand, workers on bicycles tend to work more erratically and are often topping up insufficient primary sources of income – be that

175

a student loan or another job. They also tend to be younger UK nationals. Some workers are under so much pressure that they drop out of renting entirely and enter 'property guardian' arrangements in an effort to sidestep the escalating housing crisis. These two groups, when they cooperate, can form a strong coalition, despite their significant cultural, racial, linguistic, political, and economic differences. Women workers, however, are often excluded due to the internal culture of the workforce.

The workers' organization that emerges and re-emerges out of this technical and social class composition is characterized by a collective class antagonism on the issues of wages and conditions. In the absence of state regulation, workers have been forced to transform their invisible organization into a means for organizing collective worker resistance – or else accept an ever greater degree of exploitation.

Their favoured tactics bypass restrictive legal structures and instead rely on direct action at the point of production. This resistance tends to burst into the open whenever the situation gets worse, in what appears from the outside to be massive spontaneous mobilizations. These explosions have spread from London in August 2016, across the country, the continent, and the world, in the course of just a few years. Food-platform workers are now part of an increasingly coordinated movement that links up not only across cities and nations but also, increasingly, across different points in the supply chain. This political composition fails when the informal solidarities on which the invisible organization is based degrade, but even when this happens a new explosion is not far around the corner. If workers on the streets can form an alliance with workers in the office by going around the 'black box', they will likely access the leverage required to really challenge exploitation in the sector. In the long run, the development of platforms will likely lead to one of three outcomes: platform expropriation under workers' control as part of a wider social transformation, a fudge of 'reforms' which do little to address the problems rampant in the sector, or the total redevelopment of the platform model to increase profits (leading to couriers being forced into unemployment and poverty). Class power will be the factor which determines which of these outcomes actually takes place. The possibilities for compromise between classes remain remarkably limited.

The fight in platform capitalism has at times taken on a wider significance. Class struggle does not respect boundaries of industry, but spreads between every point at which oppressors and the oppressed come into contact. This circulation of struggle means that we can't consider one fight by one workforce in isolation. Different parts of the working class are always influencing one another. This spread of conflict isn't just a neutral process – it's a vital part of turning single, narrow disputes into wider political conflicts over the future of society. As Mike Davis puts it: 'the workers' movement can and must confront the power of capital in every aspect of social life, organizing resistance on the terrains of the economic, the political, the urban, the social-reproductive, and the associational. It is the fusion or synthesis of these struggles, rather than their simple addition, which invests the proletariat with hegemonic consciousness.'[2] In short, when the struggle of Deliveroo workers becomes part of a working-class movement, then its socially emancipatory potential can start to be realized.

In the crucible of technological development, the working class is not being defeated. In fact, workers are recomposing to form a new political subject – one which still has nothing to lose, and a world to gain.

The Politics of Parties and the Conditions of Struggle

It is difficult to write about the future, particularly when you're dealing with a subject as volatile as class struggle. Who, in July of 2016, would have predicted that a workers' movement in platform capitalism was about to explode into view? Or even, after the first strike, predicted that the conflict would continue to move from city to city and country to country until one small section of the working class –supposedly atomized beyond repair – had organized on a transnational scale? I didn't see it coming.

But socialist politics is premised on a specific kind of insurgent possibility. Italian workerism, the theoretical current which helped to develop the method of workers' inquiry and the theory of class composition that have shaped this book, referred to the moment of mobilization as a 'leap': from a position of relative stability, the class throws itself forward and into a new relation with the material reality surrounding it. The form of the leap is always somewhat obscure. It is possible to predict its outlines but never its specifics. Ahead of the 4 October strike, for example, I could tell that something was bubbling away. The strikes over the summer beforehand made that much clear. All that was needed was the right call to action at the right time, and then the mobilization exploded.

The self-organization of workers in conflict with their bosses has always been an integral part of the socialist movement. Marx argued that the only social force in capitalist society capable of overturning the ruling class and installing a new form of free society is the working class. No one is coming to the rescue – we have to do it for ourselves.

Karl Kautsky, the guiding theorist of the European socialist movement in the period before World War One, often expressed an idea called the 'merger formula', which attempted to capture the relationship between the struggle of the working class and socialist politics. Fundamentally, the socialist movement relies on two parts. The first is the struggle of the working class against exploitation, and the second is a critique of capitalism and a socialist programme. Only when these two parts advance together can everyday resistance develop into a process of social transformation.[3]

Workerism was also based on the perception that, by the early 1960s, a gap had opened up between the 'politics of parties' and the 'conditions of struggle' in Italy. The merger was coming undone, because the workers on the shop floor were advancing a political composition that didn't fit with the politics expressed by the big left-wing parties. It was in response to this gap that they proposed the method of workers' inquiry.[4] The role of workers' inquiry is to understand this divide between the two and seek to push forward a political composition which can recompose the class around a common strategy for confrontation with the ruling class.

Today, in the UK, we can see a new gap – but, this time, in the inverse form. The political composition being advanced by the Labour party seems to be ahead of the class struggle on the ground. One of the historic roles of the Labour party has been to restrict and moderate the demands of shop-floor workers for social transformation. In these circumstances, that no longer seems to be the case. Instead of workers being far ahead of the party, action in the workplace is at a historic low. The question of the relationship between the conditions of struggle in workplaces and communities and the politics of parties, therefore, has taken a new form. Workers' inquiry, as pursued here and elsewhere in publications like *Notes from Below*, allows us to look at the gap between the two that is evident in the UK, and to begin to determine what kind of political programme could achieve a merger of socialist politics and the workers' movement in our context today.

Birdsong

It's widely accepted that we live in a period of crisis. It is over a decade since the capitalist crisis of 2007–8, and life in the UK has yet to return to 'normal'. Social war waged from above under the guise of 'austerity' has led to 14 million workers living in poverty. Exploitation in the workplace has become more aggressive, as bosses have made workers sweat harder for longer for less money. The housing market continues to force millions to spend most of their wages renting uninhabitable flats. Friends and family die in hospital corridors during the annual NHS crisis. Children turn up at school hungry.

The homeless are left in the cold. The disabled go without support. The elderly go without care.

However, for a crisis to really change everything, it's not enough for the lives of the working class to get harder. The ruling class also has to be unable to continuing ruling as it has done before.[5] We are in such a crisis. Everywhere you care to look, the limits to this form of society are appearing: the ongoing process of late-stage ecological collapse, the formation of an international multi-billionaire oligarchy, and the declining global rate of profit. Our current social and economic system is hitting the buffers.

But, as the crisis grinds on, the struggle of everyday people against a system that beats them up remains mostly isolated and individual. Those workers who are involved in struggles are going against the tide. Levels of strike action in the UK are historically low, with only 33,000 workers going on strike in 2017 – making it the quietest year since records began in 1893.[6] Likewise, social movements are quiet after the surge of 2011–15.[7] This isn't only a UK phenomenon – across the fifteen core countries of the EU, levels of days not worked due to strikes fell by 40 per cent from the 1990s to the 2000s.[8] In order to change the balance of class forces within our society, an insurgent workers' movement would have to burst into the open.

Just in Brighton, it's possible to perceive the outlines of what that insurgent movement could look like. As I write, in November 2018, the Wetherspoons workers have just won themselves a pay rise after their first ever strike, and are now looking to organize new workplaces. The renters' union in the city, ACORN, is calling weekly pickets outside letting-agent offices to force slum landlords to make repairs and return deposits. Community foodbanks, cafes, language schools, and boxing clubs are building infrastructure in the gaps the state has left behind. Meetings, reading groups, and discussions of socialist politics are taking place almost every day throughout the city. This is nothing like the intensity of working-class self-organization that would be necessary to successfully implement a socialist programme – but it is evidence of a continued subterranean process of organization that could explode into action, should the right circumstances arise. And, still, the turquoise boxes flash back and forth below my window. But whilst the multi-faceted crisis facing us today might look increasingly serious, crisis alone is no guarantee of socialism. Capitalism has survived these kinds of moments before.

In 1915, Rosa Luxemburg was in a German prison. The socialist leader was imprisoned because she opposed the remorseless slaughter of World War One. She was seeing first-hand how inter-imperialist rivalry and the instability of the capitalist system was leading to the deaths of millions of working-class people for no purpose at all. In prison, she wrote *The Junius Pamphlet*, in which she reflected on a phrase from Friedrich Engels, Marx's close friend and editor: '"Bourgeois society stands at the crossroads, either transition to socialism or regression into barbarism." Until now, we have all probably read and repeated these words thoughtlessly, without suspecting their fearsome seriousness. A look around us at this moment shows what the regression of bourgeois society into barbarism means.'9

From her cell, one of her only precious sources of hope was in the birdsong beyond the bars. That contrast, between birdsong and artillery, between socialism and barbarism, has defined the century since. Barbarism, in the form of the interlinked forces of fascism and capitalism, has sometimes won out. But socialism, itself also taking many varied forms, endures. Today, rather than columns of workers being marched to die in a futile war, boats full of refugees are being launched from the shores of Libya. We are at the crossroads again. But we can also hear the birdsong.

All the workers who have been the subject of this book have played a role in the fight against barbarism. The workers' movement, organized in both the workplace and the community, is the only social force that can provide the class power and the political leadership required to turn socialism from a pipe dream into a reality. That process of transformation is not a simple one. Winning an election on a left-wing platform isn't the end of the struggle – it's just the start. Billionaires will fight back – and, in the end, the balance of power in the streets matters more than the balance of power in parliament. Platform workers, a segment of the working class currently leading a struggle against immiseration at the leading edge of capitalist development, may come to play a definitive role in building that power.

The stakes could not be higher. We face an increasingly dangerous world without any guarantee that we will win – but that doesn't mean that birds don't sing.

Notes

1 Introduction

1 I. Smith, D. Blood, and Æ. Rininsland (2018) The FT 1000: the complete list of Europe's fastest-growing companies. *Financial Times*. 11 February. https://ig.ft.com/ft-1000/2018.
2 M. Murgia (2017) Deliveroo secures $385m in funding. *Financial Times*. 23 September. www.ft.com/content/bc26aaaa-a06b-11e7-b797-b61809486fe2.
3 Deliveroo reveals cost of doing business (2017) *BBC News*. 21 September. www.bbc.co.uk/news/business-41347817.
4 C. Hodgson and A. Ram (2018) Deliveroo losses widen as food delivery app invests in expansion. *Financial Times*. 1 October. www.ft.com/content/c50d0766-c565-11e8-bc21-54264d1c4647.
5 K. Marx (1967) *Capital*, volume I, 4th edn. International Publishers, p. 166.
6 K. Marx (1880) *A Workers' Inquiry*. Marxists.org. www.marxists.org/archive/marx/works/1880/04/20.htm.
7 F. Engels (2009) *The condition of the working class in England*. Penguin.

184

8 Marx, *Capital*, volume 1.
9 A. Haider and S. Mohandesi (2013) Workers' inquiry: a genealogy. *Viewpoint.* www.viewpointmag.com/2013/09/27/workers-inquiry-a-genealogy.
10 For more on the class composition framework and its historical development, see J. Woodcock, S. Wheeler, J. Thorne, C. Cant, A. Marotta, and L. Hughes (2018) The workers' inquiry and social composition. *Notes from Below.* www.notesfrombelow.org/article/workers-inquiry-and-social-composition; S. Wright (2002) *Storming heaven: class composition and struggle in Italian Autonomous Marxism.* Pluto Press.
11 F. Fukuyama (2012) *The end of history and the last man.* Penguin Books.
12 M. Roberts (2016) *The long depression.* Haymarket Books.
13 M. Fisher (2009) *Capitalist realism: is there no alternative?* Zero Books.
14 N. Srnicek (2017) *Platform capitalism.* Polity.
15 J. Woodcock and M. Graham (2019) *The gig economy: a critical introduction to platform work.* Polity.
16 Some estimates claim that 2.8 million people worked in the gig economy at some point in 2017. Of these, 700,000 earned below the living wage whilst they did so, and 21 per cent worked for food-delivery platforms. This would imply that around half a million workers worked for a food platform at some point in 2017, which intuitively seems very high. See R. Booth (2018) 700,000 gig workers paid below national minimum wage. *Guardian.* 7 February. www.theguardian.com/business/2018/feb/07/death-dpd-courier-don-lane-tragedy-business-secretary.
17 For an analysis of how this kind of cutting-edge organizing and inquiry actually took place in the early tech industry, see E. Brophy (2006) System error: labour precarity and collective organizing at Microsoft. *Canadian Journal of Communication* 31.

18 R. Edwards (1979) *Contested terrain: the transformation of the workplace in the twentieth century*. Heinemann.
19 A. Rosenblat, and L. Stark (2016) Algorithmic labor and information asymmetries: a case study of Uber's drivers. *International Journal of Communication* 10.
20 D. Feenan, (2018) The birth of the strike. *Jacobin*. http:// jacobinmag.com/2018/05/strikes-history-london-sailors-coal-heavers.
21 Marx, *Capital*, volume 1, p. 712.
22 W. Benbow (1832) Grand national holiday and congress of the productive classes. Marxists.org. www.marxists.org/history/england/chartists/benbow-congress.htm.
23 S. Hall (1990) The great moving right show, in S. Hall (ed.), *The politics of Thatcherism*. Lawrence and Wishart.
24 D. Harvey (2005) *A brief history of neoliberalism*. Oxford University Press.
25 Hall, The great moving right show.
26 D. J. Bailey (2014) Contending the crisis: what role for extra-parliamentary British politics? *British Politics* 9.
27 R. Partington (2018) UK worker strike total falls to lowest level since 1893. *Guardian*. 30 May. www.theguardian.com/uk-news/2018/may/30/strikes-in-uk-fall-to-lowest-level-since-records-began-in-1893.

2 The Job

1 C. Cant (2016) 5 things you need to know about the UberEATS strike. *Novara Media*. https://novaramedia.com/2016/08/25/5-things-you-need-to-know-about-the-ubereats-strike.
2 K. Marx (1967) *Capital*, volume I, 4th edn. International Publishers, p.172
3 C. Bossen (2012) The Chicago Couriers' Union 2003–2010: a case study in solidarity unionism. *WorkingUSA* 15.

3 The System of Control

1 R. Edwards (1979) *Contested terrain: the transformation of the workplace in the twentieth century*. Heinemann.

2 F. W. Taylor (2014) *The principles of scientific management*. Martino Publishing.

3 H. Braverman (1975) *Labor and monopoly capital: the degradation of work in the twentieth century*. Monthly Review Press.

4 K. Marx (1967) *Capital*, volume I, 4th edn. International Publishers, p. 313.

5 A. Rosenblat, and L. Stark (2016) Algorithmic labor and information asymmetries: a case study of Uber's drivers. *International Journal of Communication* 10.

6 H. Garlick (2017) Dark kitchens: is this the future of takeaway? *Financial Times*. www.ft.com/content/d23c44 fe-4b0b-11e7-919a-1e14ce4af89b.

7 S. Usborne (2018) What is the true human cost of your £5 hand car wash? *Guardian*. www.theguardian.com/world/ 2018/jul/16/true-human-cost 5 pound-hand-car-wash-modern-slavery.

8 D. F. Noble (2011) *Forces of production: a social history of industrial automation*. Transaction Publishers.

9 Noble, *Forces of production*, p. 84.

10 Noble, *Forces of production*, p. 231.

11 H. Braverman (1975) *Labor and monopoly capital: the degradation of work in the twentieth century*. Monthly Review Press, p. 206.

12 Marx, *Capital*, volume 1, ch. 21.

13 Quoted in G. Hanlon (2016) *The dark side of management: a secret history of management theory*. Routledge, p.105. For more on development of job differentiation and piece rates in early twentieth-century industry, see K. Stone (1974) The origins of job structures in the steel industry. *Review of Radical Political Economics* 6.

14 B. Silver (2003) *Forces of labour: workers' movements and globalisation since 1870*. Cambridge University Press.

15 T. Cliff (1970) *The employers' offensive: productivity deals and how to fight them*. Pluto Press.

16 H. Beynon (1973) *Working for Ford*. Allen Lane, p. 20.

17 N. Christie and H. Ward (2018) *The emerging issues for management of occupational road risk in a changing economy: a survey of gig economy drivers, riders and their managers*. UCL Centre for Transport Studies.

18 M. Escalante (2018) The perilous gig economy: why Caviar must pay for bike courier's death. *Philadelphia Partisan*. https://philadelphiapartisan.com/2018/05/17/the-perilous-gig-economy-why-caviar-must-pay-for-bike-couriers-death.

19 Marx, *Capital*, volume 1, p. 401.

20 F. Pasquale (2015) *The black box society: the secret algorithms that control money and information*. Harvard University Press.

21 M. Glaberman (2002). *Punching out & other writings*. C. H. Kerr Publishers.

22 D. Montgomery (1995) *The fall of the house of labor: the workplace, the state, and American labor activism, 1865–1925*. Cambridge University Press, p. 224.

23 Hanlon, *The dark side of management*.

24 Taylor, *The principles of scientific management*.

25 K. Legge (1989) HRM: a critical analysis, in J. Storey (ed.), *New perspectives on Human Resource Management*. Routledge.

26 M. Noon (1992) HRM: a map, model or theory? in P. Blyton and P. Turnbull (eds.), *Reassessing Human Resource Management*. Sage.

27 E. Mayo (1977) *The human problems of an industrial civilization: work, its rewards and discontents*. Arno Press; E. Mayo (1923) The irrational factor in human

behavior: the 'night-mind' in industry. *Annals of the American Academy of Political and Social Science* 110.

28 R. K. Upadhya (2018) Disrupting disruption: on intervening against technological restructuring. *Notes from Below*. https://notesfrombelow.org/article/disrupting-disruption.

29 Anon. (2018) Prospects for organizing the tech industry. *Notes from Below*. https://notesfrombelow.org/article/prospects-for-organizing-the-tech-industry.

30 Marx, *Capital*, volume 1, ch. 4.

31 N. Dyer-Witheford, (2015) *Cyber-proletariat: global labour in the digital vortex*. Pluto Press.

32 Independent Workers of Great Britain CLB, and J. Woodcock (2017) IWGB evidence submission. http://data.parliament.uk/writtenevidence/committeeevidence.svc/evidencedocument/business-energy-and-industrial-strategy-committee/future-world-of-work/written/47112.pdf.

33 M. V. Gómez and C. Delgado (2018) La Inspección de Trabajo reclama a Deliveroo 1,3 millones de euros por sus falsos autónomos en Barcelona. *El País*. https://elpais.com/economia/2018/07/03/actualidad/1530606502_371980.html.

34 S. Butler (2017) Deliveroo accused of 'creating vocabulary' to avoid calling couriers employees. *Guardian*. www.theguardian.com/business/2017/apr/05/deliveroo-couriers-employees-managers.

4 A Short History of Precarious Militants

1 M. Quinlan (2012) The 'pre-invention' of precarious employment: the changing world of work in context. *Economic and Labour Relations Review* 23.

2 S. Weir (2004) *Singlejack solidarity*. University of Minnesota Press.

3 S. Hill (1976) *The dockers: class and tradition in London*. Heinemann, p. 16.
4 B. Hunter (1958) 'Hands off the blue union!' Democracy on the docks. *Labour Review* 3(1). www.billhunterweb. org.uk/articles/hands_off_the_blue_union.htm.
5 Socialisme ou Barbarie (2018) 'The English dockers' strikes', in *Socialism ou Barbarie: an anthology*. Eris, pp. 137–52.
6 P. Turnbull and D. Sapsford (2001) Hitting the bricks: an international comparative study of conflict on the water-front. *Industrial Relations*, 40(2).
7 For more on containerization from the workers' point of view, see Weir, *Singlejack solidarity*; and Hill *The dockers*.
8 D. Sapsford and P. Turnbull (1990) Dockers, Devlin and industrial disputes. *Industrial Relations Journal* 21.
9 D. Lamb (1974) The lump: a heretical analysis. libcom.org. http://libcom.org/history/lump-heretical-analysis-dave-lamb.

5 Workers and Customers

1 Nomis (2018) Labour market profile Brighton. www.no misweb.co.uk/reports/lmp/la/1946157280/report.aspx# tabempunemp.
2 Brighton and Hove City Council (2010) *Housing costs update Quarter 4 2010*. www.brighton-hove.gov.uk/sites/ brighton-hove.gov.uk/files/2010%20%284%29%20 Housing%20Costs%20%28Oct-Dec%29.pdf; Brighton and Hove City Council (2017) *Brighton & Hove housing market report Quarter 4 2017*. www.brighton-hove.gov. uk/sites/brighton-hove.gov.uk/files/2017%20%284% 29%20Housing%20Market%20Report%20%28Oct-Dec%29.pdf.

3 F. Kooti, M. Grbovic, L. M. Aiello, N. Djuric, V. Radosavljevic, and K. Lerman (2017) Analyzing Uber's ride-sharing economy, in *Proceedings of the 26th International Conference*, ACM Press.
4 K. Bryan (2019) Deliveroo and Uber Eats takeaway riders rent jobs to 'illegal immigrants'. *The Times*. www.thetimes.co.uk/article/deliveroo-and-uber-eats-takeaway-riders-rent-jobs-to-illegal-immigrants-ml36gvp93.
5 M. Perry (2000) *Bread and work: social policy and the experience of unemployment, 1918–39.* Pluto Press, p. 103.
6 A. Marotta and L. Hughes (2018) Rebellion at the LSE: a cleaning sector inquiry. *Notes from Below.* https://notesfrombelow.org/article/rebellion-lse-cleaning-sector-inquiry.
7 R. Cavendish (1982) *Women on the line.* Routledge; A. Pollert (1981) *Girls, wives, factory lives.* Macmillan; S. Westwood (1984) *All day, every day: factory and family in the making of women's lives.* Pluto Press.
8 See New Syndicalist (2019) No love for Deliveroo! *New Syndicalist.* https://newsyndicalist.org/2019/02/15/manchester-deliveroo-strike.
9 M. Fisher (2014) Good for nothing. *The Occupied Times.* https://theoccupiedtimes.org/?p=12841.
10 S. Surette (2018) Perks of the job. *Notes from Below.* https://notesfrombelow.org/article/perks-of-the-job.
11 N. Khomami (2017) UK's appetite for gourmet takeaway fuels restaurant delivery boom. *Guardian.* www.theguardian.com/lifeandstyle/2017/mar/03/restaurant-takeaway-delivery-boom-uk-deliveroo-ubereats-food.
12 Quoted in P. Sotiris (2018) Poulantzas revisited: state, classes and socialist transition; an interview with Panagiotis Sotiris. *Viewpoint Magazine.* www.viewpointmag.com/2018/05/07/poulantzas-revisited-state-classes-and-socialist-transition-an-interview-with-panagiotis-sotiris.

6 The Strikes

1 M. Tronti (2013) *Operai e capitale*. DeriveApprodi, p. 37.
2 A. Bogg (2016) Beyond neo-liberalism: the trade union act 2016 and the authoritarian state. *Industrial Law Journal* 45.
3 R. Warin (2017) Dinner for one? A report on Deliveroo work in Brighton. *Autonomy Institute*. http://autonomy. work/wp-content/uploads/2018/08/Deliveroo-03.pdf.
4 F. W. Taylor (2014) *The principles of scientific management*. Martino Publishing.
5 BREAKING: IWGB response to the Taylor Review (2017). Independent Workers of Great Britain. https://iwgb.org. uk/post/5aa706668a4cb/breaking-iwgb-response-to-the-.
6 F. Waters and J. Woodcock (2017) Far from seamless: a workers' inquiry at Deliveroo. *Viewpoint*. www.view pointmag.com/2017/09/20/far-seamless-workers-inquiry -deliveroo.
7 J. Gapper (2018) The food app revolution will eat its drivers. *Financial Times*. www.ft.com/content/e0d612e0-c0b9-11e8-95b1-d36dfef1b89a.
8 Gapper, The food app revolution will eat its drivers.
9 New normal? Strike Map shows steady trends in worker actions in first half of 2017 (2017) *China Labour Bulletin*. https://clb.org.hk/content/new-normal-strike-map-shows-steady-trends-worker-actions-first-half-2017.
10 O. Wang (2019) China's gig economy losing ability to absorb laid off factory workers. *South China Morning Post*. www.scmp.com/economy/china-economy/article/ 2185789/chinas-grey-economy-losing-ability-be-employ ment-backstop-laid.
11 China's food delivery workers take a stand (2017) *China Labour Bulletin*. https://clb.org.hk/content/china%E2% 80%99s-food-delivery-workers-take-stand; Multiple vio-

lent clashes erupt, all involving food delivery drivers (2017) *China Labour Bulletin.* https://clb.org.hk/content/multiple-violent-clashes-erupt-all-involving-food-delivery-drivers.

12 R. Alquati (2013) Trans. E. Calder Williams. The struggle at FIAT. *Viewpoint.* www.viewpointmag.com/2013/09/26/struggle-at-fiat-1964.

13 A. T. DeMaria (2014). Your nonunion employees have walked out . . . now what? *Management Report for Nonunion Organizations* 37(11).

14 A. T. DeMaria (2017) Organizers increase sophistication with digital communications. *Management Report for Nonunion Organizations* 40(2), p. 4.

15 L. Demori and P. Locatelli (2018) Massive truckers' strike exposes political chaos as Brazil gears up for elections in October. *The Intercept.* https://theintercept.com/2018/06/05/brazil-truckers-strike.

16 M. Issac (2017) One surprise standout for Uber: food delivery. *New York Times.* www.nytimes.com/2017/09/23/technology/ubereats-food-delivery.html.

17 D. Shepardson (2018) Uber 'on track' for IPO in 2019, no plans to sell tech unit – CEO. Reuters. *URL* https://uk.reuters.com/article/uk-uber-ceo/uber-on-track-for-ipo-in-2019-no-plans-to-sell-tech-unit-ceo-idUKKCN1LL2NC.

18 S. Bond, J. Fontanella-Khan, and A. Ram (2018) Uber in early talks to acquire food delivery rival Deliveroo. *Financial Times.* www.ft.com/content/dc685456-bd3b-11e8-94b2-17176fbf93f5.

19 C. Hodgson and A. Ram (2018) Deliveroo losses widen as food delivery app invests in expansion. *Financial Times.* www.ft.com/content/c50d0766-c565-11e8-bc21-54264d1c4647.

20 F. Cocco (2018) Just Eat shares fall 7% after reports Uber looking at Deliveroo. *Financial Times.* www.ft.com/content/600c8d40-bd6c-11e8-8274-55b72926558f.

21 K. Moody (2017) *On new terrain: how capital is reshaping the battleground of class war.* Haymarket Books, p. 50.

7 Looking Forward

1 S. Panja (2018) Deliveroo plans to make its own food and replace chefs and riders with robots. *Eater.* https://london.eater.com/2018/3/29/17175482/deliveroo-future-plans-robots-profits-investors.

2 S. Scott (2019) Meet Scout. Amazon. https://blog.about amazon.com/transportation/meet-scout.

3 L. A. Hamilton (2018) People kicking these food delivery robots is an early insight into how cruel humans could be to robots. *SFGate.* www.sfgate.com/technology/busi nessinsider/article/People-kicking-these-food-delivery-ro bots-is-an-12980712.php.

4 T. O'Reilly (2017) *WTF: what's the future and why it's up to us.* Harper Collins, p. 273.

5 O'Reilly, *WTF,* p. 302.

6 J. Watkins, W. Wulaningsih, C. Da Zhou, et al. (2017) Effects of health and social care spending constraints on mortality in England: a time trend analysis. *BMJ Open* 7.

7 This point is shared by J. Woodcock and M. Graham (2019) *The gig economy: a critical introduction.* Polity.

8 F. Holtwell (2018) Bringing back the Lucas plan. *Notes from Below.* https://notesfrombelow.org/article/bringing-back-the-lucas-plan.

9 UCL Institute for Global Prosperity (2017) *Social prosperity for the future: a proposal for Universal Basic Services.* www.ucl.ac.uk/bartlett/igp/sites/bartlett/files/uni versal_basic_services_-_the_institute_for_global_prosper ity_.pdf.

10 UCL Institute for Global Prosperity, *Social prosperity for the future.*

11 I. Landa (2012) *The apprentice's sorcerer: liberal tradition and fascism*. Haymarket Books.

12 G. Eley (2002) *Forging democracy: the history of the left in Europe, 1850–2000*. Oxford University Press.

13 R. Miliband (2015) The coup in Chile, in *Class war conservatism: and other essays*. Verso.

8 A New Wave

1 Anon. (2018) Spread the Spoons strike. *Notes from Below*. https://notesfrombelow.org/article/spread-spoons-strike.

2 J. Woodcock and L. Hughes (2018) The view from the picket line: reports from the food platform strike on October 4th. *Notes from Below*. https://notesfrombelow.org/article/view-picket-line-reports food platform-strike-octo.

3 J. McAlevey (2016) *No shortcuts: organizing for power in the new gilded age*. Oxford University Press.

9 Conclusion

1 R. Panzieri (2017) The capitalist use of machinery: Marx versus the objectivists. Libcom.org. https://libcom.org/library/capitalist-use-machinery-raniero-panzieri.

2 M. Davis (2018) *Old gods, new enigmas*. Verso, p. 119.

3 L. T Lih (2011) *Lenin*. Reaktion Books.

4 M. Filippini and E. Macchia (2012) *Leaping forward: Mario Tronti and the history of political workerism*. Jan van Eyck Academie.

5 V. I. Lenin (1915) *The collapse of the Second International*. Marxists.org. www.marxists.org/archive/lenin/works/1915/csi.

6 R. Partington (2018) UK worker strike total falls to lowest level since 1893. *Guardian*. www.theguardian.

com/uk-news/2018/may/30/strikes-in-uk-fall-to-lowest-level-since-records-began-in-1893.

7 D. J. Bailey (2015) Resistance is futile? The impact of disruptive protest in the 'silver age of permanent austerity'. *Socio-Economic Review* 13.

8 K. Vandaele (2011) *Sustaining or abandoning 'social peace'? Strike development and trends in Europe since the 1990s*. European Trade Union Institute.

9 R. Luxemburg (1915). *The Junius Pamphlet: the crisis of German social democracy*. Marxists.org. www.marxists.org/archive/luxemburg/1915/junius.

Index

Index